I GOT THE IDEAR

# I GOT THE IDEAR

MY LOVE AFFAIR WITH MAINE LANGUAGE

*by* Marion Kingston Stocking

With an Afterword on Maine Dialects by Pauleena MacDougall

THE MAINE FOLKLIFE CENTER

ORONO, MAINE 2007

Northeast Folklore
Volume XL 2007
Pauleena M. MacDougall, Editor

Copyright © 2007 by Marion Kingston Stocking. Afterword © 2007 by Pauleena M. MacDougall. All rights reserved under International and Pan-American Copyright Conventions. No part of this book may be reproduced, in whole or in part, by any means whatsoever, whether photomechanical, electronic, or otherwise, without permission in writing from the publisher, except by a reviewer who may quote brief passages in a review to be printed in a journal or newspaper.

The Maine Folklife Center is a non-profit organization devoted to the collection, preservation, study and publication of the songs, legends, tales and other traditions of Maine and the Atlantic Provinces of Canada. Regular annual membership is $25.00 per year. All members receive the Maine Folklife Newsletter as it appears and a subscription to *Northeast Folklore*, as well as a ten percent discount on tapes, books and videos as a privilege of membership.

*Northeast Folklore* is an annual publication issued by the Maine Folklife Center, formerly the Northeast Folklore Society. Each year the Center publishes a single fresh collection of regional material or a comparative study or several short collections or studies. Authors are invited to submit manuscripts for consideration to the Editor, Northeast Folklore, 5773 South Stevens Hall, University of Maine. Orono, Maine 04469-5773. Manuscripts are acknowledged on receipt and are evaluated first by the editor and then, if appropriate for the journal, sent to two qualified referees for review. Authors are notified as soon as a decision is made to reject, accept, or reject with the possibility for revision and resubmission. Manuscripts submitted should not have been published elsewhere or be under consideration by any other publisher.

Paper used in the publication meets the requirements of the American National Standard for Information Sciences—Permanence of Paper for Printed Library Materials, ANSI Z39.48-1984.

Book design by Michael Alpert

ISBN: 0-943197-33-3   (*Northeast Folklore*, volume XL)


The Selection from Stephen King's "The Reach" is Reprinted with Permission. © Stephen King. All rights reserved.

Cover photograph by Marion Stocking: Lee Davis and Marnie Balch [later Libby] on Spednic Lake, July, 1948.

TABLE OF CONTENTS

Foreword  ix

Preface  xi

Acknowledgments and Permissions  xiii

Chapter I. Spell-bound  1

Chapter II. So to Speak  29

Chapter III. Lit'ry Lingo  41

Chapter IV. Bah Ha Bah Barstids  49

Appendix A. University of Maine Student Spellings: 1946–1948  58

Appendix B. Katherine Heidinger, "Transplant Translates Our Dialect for Tourists"  60

Principal Sources  63

Afterword: "Dialects of Maine" by Pauleena MacDougall  65

Index  78

For my undergraduate friends at the University of Maine, 1946–1948

FOREWORD

With great pleasure I introduce to you *I Got the Idear: My Love Affair with Maine Language* by Marion Kingston Stocking. A teacher of English for most of her life, Stocking has always been fascinated by the speech of people around her. And she has joyfully collected many samples of Maine dialects from her students, as well as from friends and reading. Marion grew up in New England, in a suburb north of Boston, where she first became aware of her own New England dialect. As she describes in her first chapter, she noted a difference in speech between the Boston speakers and a neighbor from Maine who added an *r* at the end of the word *idea*. Then in college at Mount Holyoke in Massachusetts she recalls having the pronunciation of a friend corrected by a speech professor to establish a "correct" speech. Later while teaching in Maine, she collected examples of "Maine" spelling from her students, and began to notice those same spellings in historical literature, in the *Bangor Daily News*, and in menus and shop signs. Newspaper editors missed many of these misspellings. She found them in magazines and newspapers, both weekly and daily: *The Maine Organic Farmer and Gardener*, the *Maine Times*— seemingly everywhere she looked.

Stocking places many of her observations about Maine dialect in the context of her memories of teaching at the University of Maine, at a time when many soldiers returned to school on the GI Bill. Her memories of teaching English at that time relate an important time in the history of the University. She also notes the problem of class distinction in language, and the conflict between standardizers (language purists) and those who appreciate the diversity of regional dialects. Although some people stereotype social class by speech patterns, many people in Maine refuse to succumb to the prescriptive speech they hear on television and in the movies, proudly continuing to speak in their own dialect. She gives us some fine examples of the use of regional dialect by writers such as John Gould, Holman Day,

Carolyn Chute and Stephen King, who have all attempted to convey Maine speech using various methods. She also provides an important perspective on the commodification of Maine culture—in particular the use of Maine dialect as an advertising gimmick in current usage around the state.

Finally, she provides us with a list of spellings from her grade books of the 1940s at the University of Maine. They're really fun to read, and it would be interesting to compare these with those collected by an English teacher at the University of Maine today. I wonder if teachers are still finding the same kind of spellings that reflect local speech. Stocking's writing is clear, concise and entertaining and I know that you will enjoy reading what follows as much as I have.

—PMM

## PREFACE

Although I studied under a woman who had worked on Hans Kurath's great *Linguistic Atlas of New England*, I am not otherwise trained as a linguist. I am by nature a squirrel, a compulsive collector. When I started this project I thought it was going to be about Maine spelling. But I stumbled over the line between spelling and pronunciation and fell kersplash into this book. I hope it is clear that my attraction to the subject is driven by my love affair with the great regional diversity of languages. I grieve at the attrition of ancient languages throughout the globe along with the rich cultures they express. In my own region I regret the homogenization of New England dialects and their decline into mere subjects for entertainment or commercialization. This book is intended as a tribute to these regional voices as they have enriched my life.

I should like to assure any scholar who may happen on this little book that I have invented or exaggerated nothing in these pages. It would please me if my compulsive collections would serve as source material for and memorial to how folk talked back in the days before we all sounded the same.

Since my primary source is my own experience with Yankee lingo, the chapters follow a roughly autobiographical track—like the good old railway of my childhood, the Boston and Maine.

–M.K.S., Lamoine, Maine, January 2007

ACKNOWLEGMENTS AND PERMISSIONS

I would like to thank those GI Bill veterans in my classes in the forties for starting me on this track. I am grateful as well to the fine Maine fiction writers, essayists, and columnists who appreciate their linguistic heritage and honor it in their writing. For permission to quote their words I thank these writers and their publishers: Earl Brechlin, William Carpenter, Carolyn Chute, Paul Doiron, John Gould, Katherine Heidinger, Stephen King, Ruth Moore, and Sanford ("Sandy") Phippen. To Pauleena MacDougall and Sandy Ives, thanks for their editorial support and to the former especially for her generous Foreword and Afterword. Finally, but not least, gratitude to those friends and relations, not otherwise acknowledged, who have contributed their discoveries to this endeavor: Hilda Fife, Burt and Marnie Libby, Nancy Nielsen, and especially Fred, Anne, and Andy Stocking.

# I. Spell-bound

# 1.

Oh, it was memorable! Blood in my eyes, down my face, pulsing all over the new hall wallpaper. Arterial hemorrhages are spectacular. Here's the picture: I was eight and had skidded on some acorns while running up the front walk to our Dutch Colonial house in a bedroom suburb north of Boston. My forehead cracked against the corner of one of the brick pillars by the front steps. Next day I went to school with a dramatic bandage.

"Hey, what happened to you?"

"I hit my head on a pillar."

Hysterical laughter: "You hit your head on a piller?"

"Not that kind of a piller, dummy, a brick piller."

"Gee, at my house we've got feather pillers."

I remember this—oh, how I remember this—as my first awareness of the regional dialect I was being raised to. Carolyn T. Daniels tells of an "important and corpulent" Dr. Maitland Alexander who, while chatting with a Mrs. Chapman, referred to himself as "a pillar of the church." Mrs. Chapman promptly replied, "You mean a bolster, don't you?"

My hemorrhage was traumatic for my mother, but had she understood the implications she should have been proud. My parents were of German-speaking immigrant families, upwardly mobile in the classic second-generation tradition, in full flight from anything Germanic. World War One had intensified their revulsion; indeed, my father had legally changed his name from William Kaiser to William Kingston. They recognized a Boston suburb as the ideal place for my sister Barbara and me to grow up as young ladies speaking proper English.

Barbara and I received elocution lessons, yes we did. I can still recite some of the exercises. "I hahf to lahf to see the cahf go down the pahth to take a bahth." No arrangement of letters today can deliver the exact delicate poise of the *a* that came so easily then, but I can still hear a ghost of an *r* after the vowel.

Later came the line that visitors from away requested: "I pahked the cah in Hahvad Yahd." Here you will notice not only the throaty vowels (*park* to rhyme with *lock*) but the absence of four *r*s. You can get an approximation of the correct tone in this note that someone named "L.H.R." sent to the *New York Times* for 6 March 1943:

> The Boston children on the shore were throwing darts at a target.
> "What you doing?" called the Boston child in the canoe.
> "Playing dots," they answered.
> "Playing what?"
> "Dots."
> "Oh! Dots."
> And when a traveler in the Boston subway asked, "Does this train go to Park Street?" his fellow-passengers looked blank until he spelled it out for them—"P-A-R-K, Park." They understood his foreign pronunciation then and assured him that he was on his way to Pock Street all right.

Only recently I heard a Boston announcer on public radio explaining how the "Big Dig" was replacing the "ah-t'ry." Aha! Now I know: I had cut an "ah-t'ry" on that brick pillar. And I today take great pleasure in hearing those *r*s rearrange themselves in New England speech.

# 2.

I have no formal evidence from those days before tape recorders of how I actually spoke. But writing this has sharpened my auditory memory. I recall as a child being told that a foreign visitor who did not understand English said that the most beautiful English word he had heard was *cellahdoah*. Had he been listening, let's say, in Chicago, he would probably not have nominated *cellar door* for that honor. But to me it seemed just right, rather like the lovely sound of *Shenandoah*.

After the film of *Little Women* some reviewers wondered why the girls called their mother "Marmee." Why? Because that's the way we pronounced "Mommy."

Scholars working to reconstruct Elizabethan pronunciation have relied heavily on rhyming words. I can produce two rhymes from my early days to testify to my early speech. At summer camp in New Hampshire we had a wonderful black cook, Mrs. Kate Donaldson. She had been a cook at the Pahkah House in Boston and made Pahkah House rolls on Sundays. When she produced one of her culinary triumphs we burst into song:

Oh Katie, we love you, oh Katie so dear,
If you think we don't love you, it's a foolish idear.

I can still hear those hard *r*s clearly. What's more, I have a copy of a poem I wrote for the school magazine, ending with this, to my ear, perfect rhyme (*wan* certainly from Keats):

> The ashes of autumn are dead and wan,
> And the grey wind coughs in the uncut corn.

Not *worn* and *corn*, but *wan* and *cahn*.

# 3.

Not everyone in my neighborhood spoke proper Bostonian. Mrs. Walters down the street was from Maine. She came down hard on the *r* at the end of *idear*. She was the only person I then knew who said *ayuh*—an affirmative virtually unpronounceable by anyone not born to it. Her *ah* when she said *gahden* or *fahm* was higher in pitch and tighter than the Bostonian open-throaty *ah* of *dots*.

We had another authority for Maine speech. Every week on the radio Fred Allen took his stroll down Allen's Alley, interviewing such ethnic stereotypes as the southern Senator Claghorn and the Jewish Mrs. Nussbaum. Right down the alley was Titus Moody from Maine, played by Parker Fennelley—an ancestor of Marshall Dodge and Robert Bryan as "Bert and I."

# 4.

Then I went away to college—still in New England, to Mount Holyoke in the Connecticut Valley. Holyoke had a prescriptive speech department, and if our accent did not pass muster we were condemned to remedial reconstruction. John Gould, writing for *The Christian Science Monitor*, recalled fondly his Bowdoin professor of "oratory and rhetoric," Wilmot Brookings Mitchell: you needed to "parss" his public speaking "clarss" before you could receive a diploma. My speech parssed (and parsed) easily at Holyoke, but I remember my indignation that a Greek friend with an elegant English upper-class accent, acquired in the best schools, was singled out for speech correction. Already I was developing my life-long cherishing of, to use what Seamus Heaney calls that "pious word," diversity.

From college I went to graduate school in North Carolina—Duke University. (I thought I was going to the South, but one of my apartment-mates, from Florida, was convinced she had chosen a school "up-north.") Right away I heard that the head of the University of Maine English Department, Milton Ellis, had recently been a visiting professor at Duke. "He seemed to be a lovely gentleman," they told me, "but we couldn't understand his brogue." *Brogue!* To a Bostonian, *brogue* meant Irish, with a connotation of bog-trotter work-shoes. There were many "brogues" at Duke, and I got so that I could easily distinguish a North Georgia mountaineer from a Louisiana magnolia queen. I knew that a person who managed to slide six phonemes into *caint* (can't) was not from "Bal'ma" (Baltimore). I loved it that there was no one Southern accent. In my memory I can still hear a bright beloved Milledgeville, Georgia, voice next to a softer voice from Cullowhee, North Carolina.

# 5.

The year I first applied for a college teaching job, 1946, was the luckiest of years for someone with only an A.B. (That's right, A.B.; Holyoke still gave its degrees in Latin. And the Duke faculty had looked over my honors thesis on Spenser and told me to skip the M.A. and go straight for the Ph.D.) Wellesley offered me $800 a year, citing such urban advantages as the Boston Symphony (but on $800, how would one afford it?). St. Lawrence University topped it at $900. Then the University of Maine in Orono lured me with a munificent $1000 (perhaps shamed into such extravagance by a recent *Satevepost* story by faculty wife Owenita Sanderlin on the impossibility of raising a family on Orono's pittance). Single and accustomed to living on my $600 Duke fellowship, I hurried to sign the contract.

Moving here in 1946 was a sort of homecoming. I had been coming to Maine since 1923, on the Bangor boat from Boston, when my father, the superintendent of Barrett Company plants in New England, brought his family along on business trips. Coming in toward Bangor today on the new throughway bridge you can still look down on the old Barrett tanks where I first came ashore in Maine as a toddler. Twenty-three years later my first address in Orono was the home of Walter Leavitt, Professor of Highway Engineering, who had done Barrett work for my father. Professor Leavitt was a man with two passions—the novels of Charles Dickens and the contours of Mount Katahdin, on which he had published a splendid monograph, *Katahdin Skylines*. My return to Maine could not have been happier. I knew at once that I was home.

In 1946 the G.I. Bill inundated universities with a tidal wave of veterans, many of whom would never otherwise have considered higher education. No one could have had a happier introduction to teaching. My students (all my age or older) were grateful not to have to go back to caulking boats and peeling pulp. They were greedy for everything I could teach. It was open admission, and the writing problems were staggering. A football player from a French-speaking family had little English. Some had acute dyslexia (though we didn't yet have the term). But they worked harder and more enthusiastically than any classes I was to have in my next four decades of teaching. I can still in my memory go up the classroom rows and recall them, one by one.

I soon learned to recognize what part of the state each hailed from by his accent (all but one were men). The speech of a man from Vanceboro was virtually Canadian. The fisherman from Hancock handled the language differently from the woodsman from Millinocket. Best of all, they spelled the way they talked. I hated to "correct" the fellow who wanted to major in "silverculture." They wrote of being "carm, cool, and collected," of dancing a "poker," of "eating peppimint," of trying to "illerstraight a story," of "buying a cosarge," of dressing in "gordy colors," of "leaving things all helta skelta," of finding dry-ki (freshwater driftwood) that looked "like corpulating catapillas." I began to collect these spellings on the back pages of my grade book. (See Appendix A for a complete list.)

# 6.

New England literature is full of examples of the itinerant Yankee *r*. These consonantal peregrinations were not random; they were thoroughly predictable. We learn from Emerson's biography that Lydia Jackson changed her first name as well as her last when she married Ralph Waldo. She knew it would either be substitute Lydian for Lydia or resign herself to the inevitable Lydiar Emerson. Her formidable aunt-to-be, Mary Moody Emerson, wrote to a relative (in Maine, actually) about "the troops quarted already here." She probably would have pronounced it *quahted*.

James Russell Lowell was especially interested in New England dialects. In 1848 he initiated *The Biglow Papers*, a series of satiric anti-war poems recited in Yankee dialect by a Mr. Hosea Biglow. In "The Courtin'" Huldy's mother sprinkles clothes "agin to-morrer's i'nin." Lowell was, however, somewhat on the defensive about what might seem an uncultured taste, and in his introduction to the second series of *The Biglow Papers* (1866) he lists for great numbers of his Yankee pronunciations comparable usage by reputable English authors. "Donne," he proclaims gleefully, "rhymes *again* with *sin*." He gives no literary examples, however, of the Yankee wandering *r*.

In 1868 a Maine writer, Charles Farrar Browne, created the character of a showman he called Artemus Ward. Browne reveled in comic spelling. Tedious as it is to read today, Artemus Ward is a goldmine of Downeast spellings: "you larf yourself to deth," "scratch orf a few lines," and "holler versiffrusly." I recognize the full flavor of the character in the ending of his business letter: "My perlitercal sentiments agree with yourn exackly. I know thay do, becawz I never saw a man whoos didn't." Browne fell into the trap of dialect writers—to misspell a spoken word (*deth, thay, whoos*) where there is no change in pronunciation.

# 7.

To get back to my Orono teaching, at first I attacked student spelling with the missionary zeal of the new instructor. I had some success with standard American misspellings:

> You wouldn't believe a lie for a minute,
> But the word believe has a lie right in it.

But Maine spellings were a different matter. A student, revising, would cross out and rewrite a problem word two or three times, and unless he went to the dictionary he often as not spelled it the way it sounded. When I noted in the margin that I was amused by *squarbell* for *squabble*, the student was offended and scribbled: "It wasn't surpose to be funny." The first paper in which I marked *morden* came back with the word "corrected" to *modren*. Later I was to receive *mordren*. *Interlectual* was improved in another paper to *interlectural*. A word like *propaganda* was infinitely misspellable. I rather like *propergander*. (At this point my spell-check is on the verge of a nervous breakdown.)

My students' attempts at correction reminded me of a graduate school friend from New York who, by years of rigorous self discipline had (alas) eradicated from her speech nearly every trace of a Brooklyn accent. One day I heard her with a friend requesting "adjourning rooms." "You mean *adjoining*?" I tactlessly suggested. "Heavens no," she replied. "That would be just like saying *goils*." At Orono I suddenly realized that in asking my guys to change their spelling I was inadvertently implying that they should change their accent. Oh, no! I loved their voices and I loved their Maine spellings.

My delight in these spellings branded me as someone "from away"—a foreigner, but amusing. Faculty in other departments started bringing me papers.

—Bacteriology papers discussed "potentially dangerous oganisms" which were grown on "arga."
—Biologists wrote of "breeding arears."
—Chemists used "centergrade themometers."
—Plant scientists wrote of "cultervation."
—Political science students discussed the "dilemmer in Chiner."
—Home economics women cut out dresses from "pattens" and learned to make strawberry "shot-cake."
—A sophomore in philosophy class got down to "fundermentals" and discovered "idears" of which he'd never had any "cornception."

Old-timers on the faculty inadvertently provided more material. A bacteriology professor taught about "portable water," preparing me for the student who wrote of duck hunting from a "potable blind." When I shared my latest trophy with one senior colleague, he bristled and asked, "What's wrong with that?" But when I encountered another English Department colleague, Cecil Reynolds, thirty years later, he allowed as how he'd read an article I'd published years back on the subject and had always meant to send me his favorite undergraduate sentence: "Out lobstering he got cart with two shots."

# 8.

I tried to find some linguistic pattern to this movement of the *r*. Ease of pronunciation was not a factor. I found *ochestras* and *ochids* on the one hand and *orperations, co-orperations,* and *orpertunities* on the other. Why a *perculiar* character but a *petruding* rock in a *pecarious* position? Why did my students misspell words they had more often seen than heard: Shakespeare's "Orthello," Joseph "Starlin," Gray's "Elergy"? Perhaps a linguist could explain the paradox of predictable behavior that eludes my attempts at classification.

I began to greet each new stack of papers in the hope of bagging fresh specimens. I tried to make it clear that the writer's pronunciation was great but that formal spelling required some self-awareness. But in the end, knowing that if the "birds wobbled in their cages" the owner was not spiking their drink, and that when "the ducks came warbling across the lawn" I was supposed to see, not hear them. Many of these spellings are imaginative and worth preserving.

—*Wiltered* flowers was a fine portmanteau, combining *wilted* and *withered*.

—Should I correct or congratulate the creator of *suffercated*?

—A man who had never seen the word *caulk* had been *corking* the seams of his lobster boat for years.

—*Mummering* leaves is a nice pun.

—Does *ripperling water* carry a *purling* stream in its portmanteau?

I was "happy as a clam" when I got this sentence: "The cook in that lumber camp was such a lazy barstard he couldn't even make creamer tarter biscuits."

# 9.

I was not far into my collection of Maine spellings before I began to discover them all over. Samuel Eliot Morison, in *The European Discovery of North America: The Northern Voyages*, explains that our current *Acadia* is a corruption of *Arcadia*, a name Giovanni da Verrazzano inscribed on his map and in a 1524 letter to King Francois I. I still occasionally see a reference to Arcadia National Park (an understandable correction: the Bar Harbor area was originally named Eden).

The Maine omissions and additions of *r*s turned up everywhere. The *Bangor Daily News* wrote of the "town farthers." There were meetings in the "Grange headquaters." A "ballard singer" arrived in town. A Wild Life Commission poster at the Outing Club cabin had a picture of a white-tail and a partridge (Ruffed Grouse): "CONSERVE DEER AND PATS." My vacuum cleaner repair man noted that he'd "checked the amature."

Instead of a mall in those days we had Freese's in Bangor (according to the tape on their parcels "Probably the Largest Department Store in the U.S.A. for a City of 30,000 People"). Over its book display in 1948 they raised a rainbow-shaped sign: "ALL THE LATEST BOOKS ON HOW TO PLAY CANASTER."

As I came to travel around the state I paid attention to old maps. The brook and mountain above Spednic Lake, named "Tuttle" on new maps, showed up as "Turtle" on an old one. Down on Cobscook Bay, the Birch Islands on one map were the Bitch Islands on another. Someone asked *Ellsworth American* columnist Hale Joy why a hill in town was called Cock Hill. A little research revealed that because of all the Irish who settled there it had been named after the county in Ireland—Cork. A Rhode Island reader wrote to the *Maine Times* in 1998 that at a Maine island general store in the thirties his mother was puzzled by entries on the charge slip; she finally figured out that *armonia* was *ammonia,* and *banners* had to be *bananas.* "The island's minister," he recalled, "concluded his pastoral prayer each Sunday with an emphatic *armen.*"

# 10.

When my two-year appointment at the University of Maine expired, I received a fellowship from the American Association of University Women (AAUW) to pursue my research on the Byron-Shelley circle overseas. I settled into a London flat and spent my days in the British Museum, my evenings in the theaters. One evening I invited to dinner Martin Landau, an R.A.F. veteran who was preparing at the Royal Academy of Dramatic Art (RADA) for a theatrical career. My other guest was my drama professor from Mount Holyoke, Kathleen Lynch. The conversation went well, but after Miss Lynch had left Martin asked me a professional question: "Could she speak properly if she chose to?" Miss Lynch had what to my ear was elegantly cultivated New England speech. (Of my own accent, Martin would only volunteer that it was "colonial.")

# 11.

When my $2,000 fellowship ran out in 1950, I came home to Maine and moved in with friends no richer than I in Vanceboro until my fall teaching position at the University of Colorado. In my second year at Boulder I did a program for the university radio station and was appalled to hear what had happened to my voice. Every trace of my New England accent was gone, replaced by a flatness that caused me a profound sense of loss. No trace of Southern, no British, only a mid-Atlantic anonymity.

I went to Margaret Robb in the speech department (Freshman Speech in those days was a requirement, like Freshman English) and asked whether there was anything I could do to retrieve my native accent. Yes, there was. She instructed me in which muscles to train to create the vowel sounds I could still hear in my memory. I was capable of them, she demonstrated, but I would have to do prolonged exercises. I did work at it, and she was right—I could reclaim those beloved vowels, but at the price of great self-conscious effort and constant practice. Only by combining will power and memory could I revive a single Yankee *a*. I could think of my old elocution exercises—so easy then! But what came naturally now was to extract the *a* of *hat* and come out with: "I have to laugh to see the calf go down the path to take a bath." It was a tad sad. It was also too late; I gave up and resigned myself to a lazy throat. Twenty-six years of "proper" speech down the drain of time.

# 12.

The next thirty years teaching English at Beloit College in Wisconsin did wonderful things for my personal and scholarly and academic life. But it did nothing for my accent. Even spending every summer in Maine on Spednic Lake had no linguistic effect except to improve my proficiency in speaking loon. Even when, in 1970, my husband Dave and I came home to Maine and arranged our teaching schedules so as to spend half our time in Hancock County, I had only to open my mouth to brand myself as from away. Then there was that bitterly cold morning driving in to town. My husband remarked, "I see you dressed for the weather." "Yes," I replied, "I dug out my old cahdroy skirt." *CAHDROY!* It just slipped out—two slick syllables instead of "cor da roy." *Cord* no longer rhymed with *bored*. And I did not have to tense the correct muscles: it was all there, waiting to be released by the right environment.

Though I feel a good deal of my New England speech slithering back, I know I can never again talk like a proper Bostonian—let alone a Maine native. (The locals let you know!) What's more, it takes more than being born here to be a native. I bragged to a Maine friend that my grandson Andy was lucky enough to be a native. Ever since she has referred to him as "Biscuit," since "if the cat has kittens in the oven, you don't call them biscuits." Still, this Biscuit at age seven spelled *fortress* as *fotris*, which sure sounds native to me.

# 13.

I am fully aware that other dialects arrange their *r*s somewhat the way Mainers do. Texan Molly Ivins writes about "the bob-wire thickets of Congress." Ah, but here it would be "bahb-wire." A White Plains bus station advertises a "GOUMET BUFFET LUNCH." Scottish Jean Redpath refers to "Robbie Budnz" (Burns). A South'n accent will let you hear an "arcapella choir." Yet any one of the Maine accents sounds deliciously different from these.

Students of Maine lingo—from the Japanese professor Tsuneko Ikemiya, who has studied the tapes in the Northeast Archives of Folklore and Oral History in Orono, to Tim Sample, professional Maine raconteur—have traced our distinctive speech to early English (this according to a story in the *Bangor Daily News*, 18 August 1993). *Ayuh* is from the old British and nautical *aye* for *yes*, and you can still hear the *ai* dipthong at the beginning of the word if you're lucky enough to be listening to a native speaker. *Ahhnt* instead of *ant* for *aunt*, says Ikemiya, is from central and Eastern England in the early Renaissance. The Elizabethan *orts* for table scraps was still in use in the forties. Yes. That was when a Dover-Foxcroft woman told a friend of mine, "I'm bringing out the orts [pronounced *aughts*] to toll the rats." (The Old English use of *to toll* as to decoy or lure was, according to my *Oxford Universal Dictionary*, by 1933 a dialect word chiefly surviving in the United States.)

I've heard it said that the Englishman is branded on the tongue at birth with his class. There is some evidence that by the beginning of the nineteenth century there a superfluous *r* was the sign of a Cockney. Thanks to an article by Nicholas A. Joukovsky (in the 1978 *Keats-Shelley Memorial Bulletin*) I learned that picky critics of the Cockney School of Poets (Charles Lamb. Leigh Hunt, and—preeminently—John Keats) chuckled whenever they could find an *r* required at the end of a line to make a rhyme, as in the case of Lamb's "Farewell to Tobacco," which runs—

> Wide an acre
> To take leave of thee, tobaccer.

And Jeanne Moskal tells (in the 1996 *Keats-Shelley Journal*) about the scholar Emily Sunstein, lost on the way to the manuscript room in the British Library, asking a guard for directions. "Well, lovey," he replied, "you go to the Magner Carter and you turn left."

I can hear the broad *a* and the terminal *r* in Cockney, and I have heard the Cockney dialect preserved in an isolated North Carolina coastal community, but no Maine speaker has ever sounded the least bit Cockney to me.

# 14.

Coming back to Maine in 1970, buying a permanent home, I was curious as to what changes might have occurred in the accents I cherish. Although what I heard mostly was TV standard, I found in spelling that the old patterns survived. I learned that DICK'S CONOR STORE in Ellsworth Falls was spelled that way because that's how it was spelled in the deed. A large red-painted triangular rock in the village of Town Hill announced RED ROCKS CONER when I first spotted it in 1972. The present owner, Douglas Richardson, explains in an interview with the *Ellsworth American* that "One time a young neighbor who claimed he didn't need to remain in school painted the rock," but he spelled the corner without the *r*. "I sent him back to school," Richardson recalls, "and asked the principal to make him write Red Rock Corner 100 times." The *Maine Times* quoted from "the official text for a woodworking course in the freshman class of one of Maine's better high schools" this instruction: "clean floors, cluding connors."

The easiest way to track the persistence of pronunciation is through signs and the printed word. (The use of *r* is easy, but the distinctive vowels leave no such footprint.) So I'll start with the easy *r*s. Ads have been a fertile source. In the classifieds: "ORCHARD BATHTUB—never installed. $15," "travis rod with drapes," "men's parker, size 40, $5" (but at Unobsky's in Calais in 1965 you could get "Knee-length parkers" for $3.99).

Other newspaper ads assured me that folks were still speaking Maineglish.

—The sign at the Indian Shop in Searsport promised "souvirnirs."

—An ad in the *Maine Times* offering "DECORATORS SPECIAL. Old fish net with seine caulks" reminded me of my 1947 student "corking" his boat. (And Bob Leeman had a column in the old *Weekly Shopper* in which he gave as an alibi for missing one's deer: "I didn't cork the trigger until it was too late.")

—The IGA in Ellsworth had "avocartos" for 99 cents; the Shop'n Save had "sherbert."

—Betsy's Kitchen on Route 3 went on the market with "mordern solar home."

—The Casco Bay Store ran an ad announcing an art display by a graduate of O'Belin College.

—Wilson's in Ellsworth advertised a dollar off on "Men's Irregular Thermal Shirts Draws." That was in the seventies. Perhaps you don't recognize that item of winter underwear. If not, you won't appreciate this story from Hale Joy's "Just Pondering" column in the *Ellsworth American*: "'Twas a raw and blustery night as the poetically inclined Marine sergeant tucked the blanket tenderly about the pretty Wave in the car seat beside him. 'Ah,' he said, 'winter draws on.' The Wave drew away hastily, 'So what,' she snapped, 'is that any of your business?'" Ah, a Wave from Maine!

Among the delicacies on menus in the seventies and eighties were these:

—The Restaurant Angelholm in Calais (that we irreverently called the Angleworm) offered "Appertizers."

—The Oronoka in Orono had "Farmers cheese blintzers."

—The Ocean House in Trenton served "sirloin beef kerbarbs."

—Sing's Polynesian Restaurant in Bangor explained that their "Scorpion Bowl" was "a rare punch with touch of almond and a gardiner." Remember those floating gardenias?

—At the Pilot's Grill bar in Bangor $1 would buy a "Magaretta."

## 15.

By far the most fertile source of Maine spellings has been newspaper and magazine articles. In the seventies we had a glossy magazine, *Maine Life*, which ran an article on Maine poet Robert Peter Tristram Coffin, spelling his third name *Tristam* throughout. Sylvia M. Kursar referred to some objectionable items as "them ornery little bastids." In one issue Bob Leeman's wildlife column mentioned the ravages of "Comerants" on young salmon, and in another, "a wide swarth of great Woodcock cover cutting right through Maine's mid-section." I'm surprised he didn't use the local name for Woodcock, *Timbadoodle*.

In the seventies Ellsworth had a wonderful paper called the *Tuesday Weekly*. In it a photo caption presented the Class of 1975 at the Humpty Dumpty Nursery School in Belfast "with their mota-boards and diplomas." And W. Alan Mayo, the editor, interviewing George Mitchell, then a candidate for the Senate, quoted him as objecting to "the monica of 'spenders'" applied then as now to Democrats. Providing the "Washington County Perspective," Marc Nault commented that "trying times like these make attitudes more mecurial." And a writer for the Cooperative Extension Service warned that a spray with malathion the first week in August "will not eliminate lava of the spruce budworm." Well, we were just then suffering an eruption of those "ornery little bastids."

The role of the dear departed *Tuesday Weekly* was for a decade filled by the *Ellsworth Weekly*, a local version of the *Bar Harbor Times*, which had a column by *Tuesday Weekly* alumnus and our local certified native, Sanford (Sandy) Phippen. Sandy has a lovely Hancock accent, which occasionally can be heard in his writing: "by then my nerves were all short anyway." (Were he to go out lobstering, I'm sure Sandy would throw back the *shots*.) The Co-op Extension newsletter advised those "desiring to visit legislature" to gather at 9:15 "in the State House rotunder," and in the *Weekly's* arts section I read that in a current production "wild west paraphanalia abound."

Another source of good spellings has been *The Maine Organic Farmer and Gardener*. They didn't call it *Fahmah* and *Gahdnah*, but at least they did give us Mort Mather on insect pests in the garden: "Squashing them twist thumb and finger is really best once you overcome any squirmishness." *Squirmishness* is a brilliant twist, but I also appreciate his use of the old-fashioned *twixt* in a new spelling. Mort's wife Barbara had a useful column on "Spoons and Spiders" (You have to have been around a while to know that a spider is not another insect pest but a skillet). She shared the good news that fennel stalks' "refreshing, slightly licoricey taste was just the thing after much wine, hor d'ourvres, and large meal." Love those Mathers!

# 16.

The late lamented *Maine Times* let many a Maine spelling through its net. A movie column reviewed *Moby Dick* with Orson Welles "(who should have been Ahab) as Father Marple." A letter to the editor spoke of a reader's "Barm-Gill-yard tree."

Edgar Allen Beem wrote (startlingly!) of "the intergration of AIDS into school health curriculums." Phyllis Austin tackled that infinitely mis-spellable word *quaternary* in writing about the University of Maine's "Institute for Quarternary Studies."

That's all right, Phyllis; I've seen it spelled that way in U.M. publications. Perhaps that's the reason they've changed the name to "Climate Change Institute."

Usually the *Maine Times* was self-conscious about its spelling. It resorted to square brackets in the following story, quoting outdoor columnist Bud Leavitt:

> This very day I returned from the Narraguagas River. The water had come up 24 inches in a very short time. . . . All day long George Joy kept saying, "Dammit, I'm going to get my barse [bass] pole and go up to George Pond and catch a barse."

Because I have subscribed for thirty-odd years, the *Ellsworth American* has been my richest source of local spellings.

—A gallery holds an exhibit of "ephermeral art."

—A headline announces "Hollywood Surplants Homefires."

—Fluctuations in the blueberry crop make the image of the industry "mecurial."

—An obituary records that the deceased "was a life member of the Knights of Themopolae."

—A reporter interviewing Senator Olympia Snowe quotes her as believing that "education should be a local perogative."

—An executive with a 32-room mansion in Bar Harbor writes that he wished to preserve a home "reminiscent of Bar Harbor's Golden Error during the turn of the century."

—Donnell Pond shows up in a news story as Darnell Pond.

—A letter to the editor refers to someone as "Nummah than a hake."

—Hazel Blackstone wins a flower show award for her "calendulars."

—When he graduated as Salutatorian from Ellsworth High School, Harearl "Buzza" Moore had to ask the *American* to stop referring to him as "Buzzer." At that time (mid-eighties) the paper, I recall, always referred to Councilman Busta Moore with no quote marks.

—Frost will cause soft spots on garden veggies, which will "deteriate in a short time."

—Esther Wood, in her column "The Native," refers to her spaniel as "our young blond Corker Polly."

—The reporter for the *American* covering a meeting with Senator Olympia Snowe refers frequently to her support of the "Graham-Rudman" bill. The local lake spelled *Graham* is pronounced like the author of the bill—Senator Phil Gramm.

For years Hale Joy wrote a column "Just Pondering" for the *American* full of local chat, jokes, and outrageous puns. One week he told about the announcer who introduced the great banjoist Eddie Peabody: "'Ladies and Gentlemen, Mr. Eddie Playbody will now pee for you.' Come to think of it, imagine Mr. Peabody's chargrin."

The *Bangor Daily News* just documented in its birth announcements the arrival of a little girl named Skyulah. I'm familiar with the name Skylar, descended I assume from Schuyler, and I'm ready to bet there's a character on television named Skylar. But *Skyulah?* Only in Maine.

# 17.

Other spontaneous Maine spellings popped up all over the field, like grasshoppers in August. They were by no means the work of uneducated writers. I edit a poetry magazine, and Maine poets have often delighted me. One titled a poem "Intergers" and in another wrote this:

> There were few turtles this year
> even here on the peninsular
> where we live.

Another Maine poet gave me *subtefuge.* One from Searsmont addressed her cover letter "To whom it may corncern" Yet another addressed her return envelope to herself at "East Livimore Me." That reminded me of a long-ago article by John Gould about his father's career sorting mail on the trains. One of his colleagues didn't know what to do with a letter addressed to "Vaudeville, Maine." Mr. Gould Sr. immediately despatched it to Waterville. (Nowadays I regularly hear about the city of Vaudeville on Maine Public Radio.)

A professor at the College of the Atlantic wrote for the *Bar Harbor Times* how "the danger of science is a narrow and non-contextural focus." One of the students at the College turned in a report of "an exciting experdition." A Maine Arts Commission newsletter announced an "Intergrated Arts experience." One of our senators argued for "serverance pay" for workers. A faculty member at the University of Maine at Farmington wrote a recommendation for a colleague, citing her book, *A Varnished World.* (Actually, the world had *Vanished.*) Bill Townsend, retired biology teacher and still the editor of the valuable natural history newsletter *The Guillemot,* used to share his students' spellings with me. One spelled *purple* as *pupel.* I saw a sign by the road advertising WRINKLES. Bill assured me that was the normal spelling of winkles. The dog-whelk, he informed me, is called a *dog-wrinkle*. In his newsletter Bill himself occasionally sneaks in an *r*, as in *Cercropia moth*.

Some of these spellings require familiarity with the turf. Not long ago I received an invitation to a Gardener's Garden Party, with a brown bag lunch at "Thuyer Garden." (The garden in Northeast Harbor is called by the Latin name for cedar—*Thuya*.) An ethnographer, hired to report on Hancock County traditional domestic arts, discovered that a Bass Harbor woman carves "ida ducks and sklodas." (In the field guide the sea ducks are eiders and scoters.) A technician in the Machias Hospital lab received a tissue specimen for a biopsy with the space for "tissue source" filled in *whot*. (Go on, say it aloud. Wart, OK?)

# II. So to Speak

# 1.

Spelling can't begin to reflect the diversity of vowel sounds in the various regions of the State of Maine. An excellent introduction is Hans Kurath's *Linguistic Atlas of New England* (1939 ff. but not published complete until 1943, and then in only two hundred copies). Kurath undertook this magnificent project in 1930, during the Depression, with linguists traveling the area recording how folks actually talked. In 1971 Raven McDavid brought out a new edition. Each page is a map of New England, with the phonetic transcription of the word or phrase in question printed on the collection site. It is endlessly fascinating to someone like me who really cares about the steadily disappearing diversity of language. For example, take the dictionary word *cater-cornered*. (I'll avoid phonetic symbols.) In Massachusetts it was as I remember it: *kitty-cornered* or, more "properly," *diagonally*. In Vermont, a diphthong slides in and the *r* begins its retreat: *catty-coernerd*. In Maine the *rs* have mostly disappeared. In Lubec the interviewer heard *catty-coanad*. I suspect we could still hear that Downeast today. In Hancock County I still hear *poor* as *pu-a* or *po-a*, just as recorded in the thirties.

# 2.

Fresh in from Wisconsin in 1971 and very alert to the language, I attended an environmental congress in Portland, where I recorded the following:

—"deteriating" conditions
—"behavi'al" problems
—"confomity" to "envyonmental" regulations
—polluting "indurstry" defying the "lore" (law)
—local "gov'ment"
—"gennal"announcements.

I knew I was home.

Many words are still pronounced Maine-wise, though I can no longer imagine their being written that way: *arftah* (after), *polertics*, an *agender* at a meeting. The paved road is "the tah." A friend of mine went to the butcher for a pot roast, and when she unwrapped it she discovered a pork roast. The local mail carrier one June asked me "Got your garden in?" "Just made it." "Well, we gort ours chow-dahed (chowdered) up, but I haven't got anything planted yet." A Lubec friend says she hears "penny wrinkles" for perrywinkles, and "Harvahd [Harvard] pollock" for "harbor pollock." And Downeast in Machias I understand some lawyers refer to affidavits as "Arthur Davids." The hospital there announced "Korea Days," which turned out to be "Career Days." A sales record at the Rowantrees Pottery in Blue Hill took down my "Stocking" as "Starkey." And no one would believe that Masha Litton's name wasn't really Marcia (she actually took the name out of a passion for Russian literature).

Perhaps I was a little uneasy to overhear a plumber in my cellar holler, "Did we do that last valve?" and get the answer, "YAHReye think so."

# 3.

Maine Public Radio used to be a good source for Maine pronunciation, but except for "The Humble Farmer," I hear little nowadays that couldn't come out of Washington—a real loss. Back when MPR was new we had a wonderful announcer, Virgil Bissett. I always paid attention when Virge spoke—of the Armadeus Quartet, Martinicus Island, the cellist Yo Yo *Mar*, an athlete with an *Archilles heel.* Other speakers on the radio said *scissor-gee* (for syzygy), *draw-ring* (for drawing), a consumer *heart-line* (for hot line), and one cited the pianist Eugene Istomin who, when he's on the road, "carries his own *tuna.*" Alas, a couple of years ago I heard Keith Shortall on MPR say "the Bangor arear," then instantly correct himself to *area.* Too bad.

In 1980, when then Justice George Mitchell was being appointed to fill Muskie's seat in the Senate, he spoke on MPR about "when the carcasses were held." (OK, *caucuses.*) This inspired Marshall Dodge (of "Bert and I") to do a radio skit about the Republican carcasses, carrying the joke about as far as it could go.

When a *Maine Times* reporter refers to "Versalius, the first modern anatomy book," I assume she was taking notes over the phone. Reporters have become self-conscious and editors are getting more vigilant, but the language is still there. Maybe it was a Maine reporter who phoned in a story to the *New York Times* about a traveling exhibit which included "more than 50 works—barred from the Museum of Modern Art and the Whitney." The *New Yorker* (8 October 1979) picked up the spelling for *borrowed* and noted: "Too spicy, probably." When a young friend, Steve, from "outta-state" visited Birdsacre Sanctuary, Chandler Richmond showed off a resident Barred Owl. When Steve asked how come the owl was bad, Chandler was confused. The explanation was simple: Steve had picked up on Chandler's pronunciation of *barred.*

# 4.

Several common one-syllable words have two in Maine. When I heard a woman in the market holler "Billy, ku ME yah," I knew he'd better get back fast. I am used to *door* as *doe-ah*, and *sure* as *shoe-ah* (as compared to *show-ah* for *shore*). Gerald E. Lewis in his 1979 *How to Talk Yankee: A Guide for Tourists, Migrants, and Summer Complaints* has two favorites: "son of a ho-ah," too common, he maintains, to be considered vulgar, and his "test phrase," "kahboo-ud kaht'n." Come down hard on the first syllable, and you get a cardboard carton. An even better test of a person's skill at speaking Yankee, Lewis maintains, is "Hahdah then a ho-ah's haht."

It isn't so much the pronunciation as the usage that has caused problems with *dear*, pronounced *de-ah* (though *deer* always has the hard *r*, as in deermeat—never venison). I am quite comfortable being addressed as "deah" by store clerks, mail carriers, nurses, tollbooth collectors, and carpenters of whatever age or gender. I have always taken it as the equivalent of the British "luv," or "lovey." Marshall L. Stone, admittedly from away, wrote a column in 1983 for the *American* to protest. He described a Downeast restaurant where a) the older waitress called the customers, men and women, "deah"; b) a young black-bearded customer walked in and addressed the younger waitress, "I'll have a reglah, deah"; c) a fisherman dragged in and got this greeting from two men drinking coffee, "Don't tell me you been out hauling traps on a day like this, deah!" Stone was offended by what he took to be sexist overtones, but an Orono linguistics professor Jacob Bennett, writer John Gould, and local language authority Sandy Phippen all assured him it had no sexual implications. Not convinced, Stone concluded: "If I were a waitress, and a macho type called me deah, I'd spill coffee down his neck. And if some fisherman called me deah, I'd haul my traps and get out of there." Bill Benson, who had a column "Island Watch" in the

*Ellsworth American* for years, recalls a Los Angeles friend, "a dentist, a sophisticate, and world traveler" who accompanied him into a Downeast store and had a male clerk ask "solicitously, 'Can I help you, dear?'" Being a Californian he immediately "bristled and turned about the same color as a Tahiti sunset." Benson concluded that "for sure there is a certain amount of risk exposure when we turn loose someone from a strange culture like Los Angeles in a store in Lubec."

Another Maine pronunciation that regularly stirs up journalistic controversy is that storm that swirls around and comes in from the northeast. Practically everyone pronounces and spells it *nor'easter.* An editorial in the *Maine Times* prompted D. H. Hatch of Orono to protest: there are nor'westers but it's "no'theasters." "Bear down on the long 'o,'" Hatch advises. John Gould, who in his nineties still had a weekly column in the papers, is another old timer who insists the only proper pronunciation is "know-theaster," with the *th* pronounced as in *those*. In his *Maine Lingo* he boxes the quarter-points of the Maine compass: *know-theast, sow-theast, sou-west,* and *nor-west.*

# 5.

Even Downeast birds may be heard speaking native. Allen Sockabasin, the Passamaquoddy musician, told about driving with a buddy down a back road in his pickup. A crow hopped out into the road ahead and then turned and hopped back. "Wa'n't that crow smaht!" Sockabasin's companion remarked. "Smaht? How's that?" "When that other crow in the tree called out 'Cah, cah, cah' he got out of the road."

# 6.

I can't close this chapter on pronunciation without a few tentative words about the social implications of regional accents. I've mentioned how important an upper-class Bostonian accent was to my upwardly mobile parents. I can trace that undemocratic snobbery, with its deep economic roots, back to the British identity of accent and class. Everyone knows Bernard Shaw's *Pygmalion*, if only through *My Fair Lady*. "The rain in Spain" is the exact counterpart to my Bostonian "Hahve to lahf to see the cahf." Nevertheless, I have met several people who have reacted with distinct chagrin when I responded with appreciation of their Maine accents. I am sure I deeply offended a medieval scholar from Hancock Point whom I was delighted to encounter in Wisconsin. I was so starved to hear a truly beautiful and authentic regional voice that I think I laughed with pleasure. That, I'm afraid, was the end of that relationship.

Today I understand the ambivalence of the natives of Hancock Point about their working-class function in that highly-educated upscale summer colony. Sandy Phippen's books portray their side of the story. In "The Returned Native" chapter of his book *The Police Know Everything*, his fictional narrator Andy gets to talk with his sister Lil about their Downeast upbringing. Lil has escaped and could never come back to stay, citing the repressive puritanism, a negative world view, and, to top it all, "the feeling that we are always inferior, second-rate citizens." She notices how "Maine people out-of-state, many of them anyway, totally reject Maine, try to change their accents and so on." To this Andy replies, "And yet, the people who have moved here and adopted Maine feel awful that they're not natives. They think it's some kind of weird honor to be born here." For this corner of Hancock County, at least, Sandy has that exactly right. It hurts, but it's true.

This sense of linguistic class distinction, no matter how historically understandable, can undermine the native health of diverse dialects. Humorist Roy Blount Jr. wrote in the *New York Times* in 1980 about the supercilious way Northerners respond to his Georgia accent. They get "a strange humorous look on their faces," as though he were confessing to something—"something largely amusing, but something which, if they weren't so broad-minded . . . they might feel entitled to feel as low-down." Blount adds a parenthesis: "('I love to hear you talk,' people have actually said to my face.)" Ouch! That strikes home! He then goes on to defend, eloquently, his pride in the language he grew up in—"pore" better than the Northern "pooor," in which "you purse your lips like a rich person."

I hope that my Wisconsin acquaintance still has her delicious Hancock accent and values it for what it means; she can be proud to be a fisherman's daughter as well as a medievalist. And an odd, perhaps rude, character from away, like me, will continue to envy it.

The pronunciation or omission of *r* as a social signifier is more complicated than I am competent to discuss. I have heard that Franklin Delano Roosevelt cultivated *r* as a vowel (*feah* for *fear*), his upper-class speech reflecting British upper-class conventions. On the other hand, I understand that since World War Two, network broadcasters are more apt to be Midwestern, and cultivated articulation of the *r* now suggests correct speech.

I'll leave that debate to linguistic anthropologists. In Maine, education doesn't mean abandoning your roots. George Mitchell spoke of "carcasses" (caucuses) and predictably I loved it. Recently I was delighted, listening to our new governor, John Baldacci, speak of "lawrenforcement," or relations with "Canader," and a search for "new idears." Let's have those new idears, certainly, but let's hang on to our traditional speech. Esther Wood, a sometime schoolmarm and then university professor, was proud of her Downeast accent and vocabulary. "Perish the thought," she wrote in one of her *Ellsworth American* columns, "that there will ever come a day when we shall all speak TV English."

I'd do my part, but as Eugenio Montale has warned, tradition is maintained "not by those who want to do so, but by those who can."

Every few years *Down East* magazine runs an article on Maine speech. Paul Doiron has assembled the most recent (September 2001). He cites Maine story-teller Tim Sample and a Deer Isle speech therapist who notice that the dilution of the Maine dialect by TV and movies has not permeated all corners of the state. Young people, especially, cling to it, they agree, and out on the islands and down at any lobster co-op the tradition holds firm. Doiron lists "The 5 Worst Maine Accents of All Time," all from film and TV except Marshall Dodge, of whom he notes: *"Bert and I* sounded pretty authentic to many Maine ears, but some folks on Matinicus still say the much-missed, Yale-educated, year-round summer person never got it right." In a sidebar on how to get rid of a Maine accent Paul Doiron concludes: "Then ask yourself why you want to lose such a beautiful accent in the first place." Amen, Paul.

# III. Lit'ry Lingo

# 1.

> *Intel-lectu-a-a-lity*
> *Is quite essential, do-on't you see*
> *In an atmosphere that's lit'ry, that's lit'ry,*
> *That's really truly lit'ry.*
>
> —sung at Mount Holyoke College, ca. 1940

Paul Doiron includes in his article a collection of quotes from Maine writers to illustrate how they capture Maine speech patterns. He inspires me to prowl down my bookshelves to see what I can find about the literary use of dialect. I have already touched on early writers who have approached the problem, from James Russell Lowell to C.F. Browne's effort to reproduce every colloquial syllable in his "Artemus Ward." The closest thing to Artemus Ward's total replication of a character's speech is a popular play by "the American Ibsen," James A. Herne, whose *Shore Acres* toured the United States for five years from 1892. Herne has been called the father of American realism for the extraordinary detail of his stage instructions, the authenticity of his characterizations, and his replication of New England dialect, especially of Maine where *Shore Acres* is set. A character in Act I asks of a proposed developer, "Is thet so thet Jordan Ma'sh's [Boston department store Jordan Marsh] comin' down here to go inter business?" Another declares that he "kinder" likes to see snow at Christmas because "it kinder—I d'know—seems kinder sorter more Christmassier—somehow" (Act IV). Herne's undeviating replication of idiom and pronunciation make the text today heavy going for an actor not born to the dialect of a past century, as in "I hup Martin haint seen yuh" (Act I). I had some of this difficulty with a column Earl Brechlin wrote for the *Ellsworth Weekly* in the mid-nineties. The title of one—"I couldah bin ah contendah"—illustrates the strengths and the weaknesses of dialect writing. The strength: recording actual pronunciation, as in *contendah*. The trap: overwriting. I have to judge this by a) my own experience of the lingo, and b) the ease of reading. Here's a sample: Brechlin's Warren and Woodrow, "Down East's dream team of popular, pithy-yet-poignant pontificators," are imagining holding the Olympics in Maine.

> Warren: We'd have to find officials who could "add and divide fractions in therah heads."
> Woodrow: "Surah, we'd have ta go outa town, but we've done that beforah." And in the "triathalon," you'd "have ta run barefoot thru the snow from ah huntin' camp to an outhouse and with an open sixteen-ounce can ah Budweisah on youah head without spillin' a drop."

Most of this I can play in my ear, except for the *r* retained in *surah* and *beforah* (which I am shoe-ah I've never heard) and *ah* for the article *a* or the preposition *of* (more likely *uh*). The real problem is that the newspaper equivalent of phonetics gets downright tedious—especially if there are unnecessary misspellings, such as "jungle jim." But I find I have another problem with this kind of writing. I have a funny feeling that the characters are being ridiculed along with the accent. I love the language too much to forgive that.

Other local columnists discuss Maine speech, but rarely reconstruct it. John Gould usually rations himself to one or two Maine spellings per column. From four columns I could find only these: the "Lombard family, pronounced 'lum-b'd' in Maine"; "it warn't easy"; "By gracious, Mother, we just blew 30 acres of pertetters!" ; go down "sullah" to fetch up apples. (I have followed Gould's rule in writing this book, slipping into the idiom only when it was irresistible.) For Gould's authoritative guide to native speech, find a library that still has his 1975 *Maine Lingo: Boiled Owls, Billdads, and Wazzats.*

# 2.

Pulling down books from my Maine collection, I find that most literary writers follow John Gould in using Maine pronunciation sparingly, for seasoning. Holman Day, the first novelist to create an Egypt, Maine, in his 1921 *When Egypt Went Broke*, uses it only in dialogue, and then rarely. Here's the tavern landlord Files explaining to a drummer (traveling salesman, for my younger readers) that the widower Britt is courting a young bookkeeper at his bank. "'It's the old story, all right, Widdereritis, and a bad run of it.'"

Ruth Moore's early stories, recently republished, are ripe with Downeast language and syntax. In the book's title story, "When Foley Craddock Tore Off My Grandfather's Thumb," Grandfather was skipper of "a three-sticker from Nova Scotia." When threatening weather (*lowry* and "pretty smurry") led him to offer Foley's stalled "punkinseed" a tow home, "'I'd ruther,' said Foley, 'set out a no'theaster.'" In "Gulliver Gunn," a character named Bilbo, seeing a strange light over Medrick Island, says, "S'pos'n we v'yge down that way. . . . If anything's come to 'em down there, somebody'd ort to go over and feed the hens." When a boy gets a shock and exclaims "Geest!" and when a man says, "Hello, yourself" to a greeting, I hear those voices. In later stories she uses very little dialect spelling, instead creating the illusion that the reader is really listening in on her characters, even when they're thinking. Here's Carlisle, in *The Walk Down Main Street*, brooding about the basketball injury that crippled him:

> So now they all saw you, gimping around.
> Oh, yare, got crippled up, playing ball.
> The idea seemed to be that you'd been numb to let it happen.

The authenticity is all in the speech rhythms and the diction: *gimping*, *numb*. Only in the dragged-out "Oh, yare" (yeaaahr) does Moore use spelling to get the right bitter tone.

Sanford Phippen, in *The Police Know Everything*, is a master of Downeast dialogue, but he rarely uses spelling to recreate it. I remember, however, one example, where the character called Fat exclaims of his wife, "She is re-MACK-able, ain't she?"

In *The Beans of Egypt, Maine* Carolyn Chute uses spelling to replicate her characters' speech. Earlene's Gram says "And no *suppah!*" In addition, like Ruth Moore's Carlyle, Earlene thinks in the spelling: "Daddy's downcellah busy with his lathe."

Stephen King also creates a running sense of live Maine conversation. But instead of creating a Maine spelling, he sneaks in a note to the reader. Here's a passage from "The Reach," one of his short stories with an explicitly Maine setting:

"Wouldn't get her off [the island] 'tall unless she was in a coma," Vera said, pronouncing the word in the downeast fashion: comer. "When Stella says 'Frog,' Alden jumps. Alden ain't but half-bright, you know. Stella pretty much runs him."

"Oh, ayuh?" Annie said.

The subtlest use of Maine pronunciation is in Bill Carpenter's *The Wooden Nickel*. He also gives us the sense of really hearing his characters, but only once does he resort to Maine spelling. But that one is delicious: Lucky Lunt, his lobsterman protagonist, is fulminating about his wife's working with the local art gallery. "Now she says 'art' like the summer people, *ort*, like there's a *r* in it. Something wrong with their tongues." This one instance encapsulates the difference between the Bostonian *r* and the Downeast *ah*. And it instructs us in how to hear everything Lucky says. All this in two short sentences, without breaking character.

# 3.

Most of the writers I've selected here are native born and value their inherited speech patterns. They write the language from the inside. All the same, a writer from away can be an accurate and appreciative observer. E. B. White in his "Maine Speech" in *One Man's Meat* is more interested in diction than pronunciation, but he does comment on the difficulty of the vanishing *r*. When a friend asks "How's the famine comin' along" he has to think fast to get the word *farming*. White mentions the word *baster*, pronounced *bayster*, which he thought derived from bastard. Since my students spelled bastard either as barstid or barstard, I doubted White's folk etymology. Having dinner in the dorm with some of my Orono students, I asked whether they knew the word *baster*. When one of them said "Yes" I perked up. Ah, but he'd read it in "some book by E.B. White." John Gould's *Maine Lingo* claims *baster* refers only to large size, such as a tremendous storm (a lambaster, maybe?). See Appendix B for a Mississippian's take on Downeast expressions.

Bill Roorbach, in his memoir *Temple Stream*, admits that one of his neighbors in the book, Earl Pomeroy, is a composite character. Earl serves several functions in the narrative, one of which is to allow the author to confront Maine speech. Earl is inclined to exaggerate his dialect to taunt the author and trap him into falling into the accent and the vocabulary. When Roorbach gets trapped into admitting he's from Connecticut, Earl comments, "Lotsa money down they-uh." Then Earl finds out who Roorbach bought his house from and asks:

> "He's the schoolteacher?" *Teach-ah.*
> "I reckon so, over in Anson."
> "You *reckon so.*"
> And he'd pegged me again, caught me imitating him.

I enjoy the way Roorbach sometimes incorporates a Maine spelling into a quotation without comment ("making bee-ah") but sometimes, in self-conscious humor, appends the pronunciation with a wry wince. To Earl, again, "'I don't want ruts in the yard, you know?' *Yad*, I said, unconscious imitation." If, like me, you're from away, you can appreciate Roorbach's uncontrollable attraction to the dialect. Later he enjoys an apple grower's description of his Macs as "had and tat." You'd have to know the Maine *a* to hear that right as "hard and tart." (E. B. White had this problem, hearing *famine* for *farming*.) All of us who write for the general reader have to accept the limitations of approximating a vowel without the use of phonetic symbols.

# IV. Bah Ha Bah Barstids

# 1.

I have moved from the spontaneous, unselfconscious speaking and spelling of my 1946 G.I. Bill students to the most linguistically aware and artful writers. In the seventies and eighties, most of the journalistic and advertising examples I have found were still not "surpose to be funny." Though I may laugh, it is not at the writer. I honor the integrity of speaker and speech. Since the end of the eighties, on the other hand, I have discovered very few unselfconscious misspellings. To my sorrow I now hear the traditional Maine accents very rarely. My collection has developed an archaeological dimension.

Along with the rapidly vanishing authentic sources, I've compulsively collected occasions of what remains—self-conscious use. Of course *Bert and I* would be a prime example. The reason Marshall Dodge has been so appreciated by Maine folks is that he clearly loves the language that he is cultivating. Our laughter is the laughter of delight at good stories well told.

Here are some further self-conscious uses of Downeast lingo:

—James Russell Wiggins, in a Christmas poem accompanying a photograph of a partridge in a birch tree:

> Perhaps he drops the pear tree
> In the myth in which he stars
> As easily as folks in Maine
> Drop out the partridge "r's."

—In R. P. Blackmur's *Sea Island Miscellany* the poet follows his line "and the han breaks heavy wings and calls" with this footnote: "'han' or 'great han' is the Maine coast familiar form for heron."

—For a while there the *Maine Times* had a calendar heading KULTCHA.

—A "back-of-the-book" essayist in *Maine Times* felt her sunny vacation smile wear off "on the plane back to Portland. A Mainah I remained."

—Down St. George way, in Tenant's Harbor: a car in a yard with its name painted on it—TINKA TOY; outside the general store at Port Clyde—a waste barrel labeled LA GABAGE. The former may be authentic, but the latter is commercial cute. (A sign on the front of that store advertised NATIVE ICE CUBES.)

Can you take a few more?

—William E.("Bo") Yerxa II wrote to the *Ellsworth American* as "A Native Mainiac whose work has recently (and temporarily) taken me 'outtastate'," but as "an educated consumer of printed data who is generally considered to have a fair amount of 'smaats'."

—A Bucksport chemistry teacher, photographed with a flock of pink flamingos impersonating Santa's reindeer, declared, "It's lawn ahhht; that's Maine talk for art."

—The *Maine Times* plugged "Maine hyoo-mah" at a story-teller's festival, and it announced the coast open for clamming, "both for the 1,500 commercial diggers and those who want a peck for suppah."

—*Down East* reported Freeport's "Great Chowdah Challenge."

—I rather like two Maine vanity plates I've spotted recently: JENI-FA is one; the other, on a pink sedan in Hallowell, PANTHA.

—A 2005 vanity plate in Ellsworth announced itself as
T8ER BUG.

The *Bar Harbor Times* has a cartoonist, Bruce Munger, who titles his box "Nor'east," though I don't think he'd say "Nor'east Creek" or "Nor'east Harbor." Off and on he deals with the missing *r*. In one drawing the sign over a shop says BA HABA BABA SHOP, and in the window is a scissors clipping the *R* off of *HAIR*.

## 2.

Headline and caption writers are especially susceptible to this self-conscious playing around. Here are four from recent *Ellsworth Americans*. "Guests enjoyed a cruise around the 'hahbah'" on the Union river. The "Garden Path" column suffered this headline: "Put up Ya Winta Squash, Deah." A photo of Tim Sample was captioned: "JUST DOWN THE ROAD FROM MOODY'S DINAH... ." And another caption announced "A Lobster Dinnah to the Winnah!" I don't how that writer missed *Lobstah*.

And while we're on seafood, Ruth Moss (pronounced Morse) told me about overhearing people in a card shop asking for a *cod* and being told they didn't sell fish. (Must have been from Boston, where they play *dots*.) A 1988 cartoon by Bousquet showed a nurse addressing a bearded patient with a pile of fish beside his bed: "WE REALLY MUST DO SOMETHING ABOUT YOUR GET-WELL CODS, MR. STEDMAN!" So I wasn't surprised this year to receive a birthday card featuring on the front a fish with a bunch of balloons, and inside "Hope you like your birthday cod." I need to point out that the pronunciation *cod* can refer either to a fish, a birthday greeting, or a measure of firewood. But the vowel sounds are delicately different, as the character in the cahd shop should have known.

Had enough? I'll close this set with a pair of Hale Joy's classic "Just Pondering" puns: "By now I'm sure you know what a fish with two knees is called. Well, silly, it's a tuny fish. And the deer without eyes is known as no idear."

# 3.

That birthday cod leads me to this chapter, on the commercial exploitation of traditional Maine speech. Self-consciousness to the max. I see the Winthrop-Atkins Co. has a line of "Cape Cads." In June watch for the sign in front of Macdonalds in Ellsworth: LOBSTA ROLLS ARE HEAH AYUH. Lobstah dinnahs and chowdah suppahs are everywhere. Reny's has an Easter "Egg Stravaganzer" Sale. You can order a "Pa'tridge Vest" from L.L. Bean. A furniture store says "'MONOVA" (come on over). Associated Hardware's mascot is a beaver, "Able Bilda." The Trenton Legion Hall has "Supah BINGO," and runs a "Supah Fishbowl Ice Fishing Derby." A sign on Ellsworth's High Street last summer read:

BAH HA BAH
STRAIGHT AHEAD.

"BAH HAHBAH" sweatshirts were all over town that year. To get the full flavor of the Bar Harbor tourist scene, check in at Geddy's Pub. There you can order "Lobsta Roll," "Clam Chowda," and "Ba HaBa Gullwings." For refreshment, look for the sign with a cocktail glass and an arrow pointing to "BA!"

Back in 1980 someone at Tardif Jeweler in Vaudeville had an exuberant copywriter. His ad went like this:

"What would a man hafta pay for this here $500 djymint?"
"Well, I tell you what, son, you're a nice lookin' young feller, just stahtin out in life, stahtin to go with a girl an' all, tell you what I'm gonna do. $500 takes it away."
*No need to dicka at Tahdif's.*

Back in the nineties a South Portland outfit created "BIG T CAHDS"—"Wicked easy" postcards by "Mainahs" for tourists who don't have time to write. A card with a moose on it has a pre-printed message that ends: "Maybe the folks signin' below have seen or will see one. They ah havin' a wondaful Maine advencha, thinkin' o' you and wish you were heeya. They also enjoy hearin' a bit o' this Maine accent heeya and theya."

The winner in the "commercial cute" category may well be this bumper sticker:

> MAINE
> BUMPAH
> STICKAH
> (FOR THE CAH)

complete with boxes in the lower corners for "MAINE REGISTRATION STICKAH."

I have heard of a Lewiston company called "Native Maine'ah™" with the motto, "We don't know any better."

# 4.

Traditional life and language are so easily copied, parodied, travestied, and exploited that today it takes a sharp ear to distinguish between what's authentic and what's derivative. I have a friend who comes from Calais, on the Canadian border, with a very subtle accent. But when he is dealing with tourists he can drop easily into the Bert-and-I Maine voice. I know a poet who can also put on the accent perfectly. But I confess I'm homesick for the days when there were as many Maine speech patterns as there were regions in the state. I wish I could remember where I heard about a Maine linguist, a college professor who claimed he could tell a person's home town by his speech. The story went that he was serving as an officer in World War One and on a cold night called an orderly to ask if he might have a fire. The orderly replied, "I'll go manufacture up some kindling." "You're from Bowdoinham, aren't you?" the officer asked, to the astonishment of the soldier, who was, of course, from Bowdoinham. The local "manufacture up some kindling" gave him away. I am nostalgic for the forties, when I could do a little of that myself, teaching veterans from all over the state, valuing that diversity that is sustained, I have to acknowledge, by class or geographical isolation.

Although I have concentrated on Maine spelling as an indicator of Maine speech, I am aware of the infinite subtleties of diction, grammar, and syntax. The books by Ruth Moore are a rich source of these qualities. And I cherish this note from John Gould's *Maine Lingo: Boiled Owls, Billdads, and Wazzats*:

> When the extremely successful (and very goo-ood!) phonograph record called *Bert and I* first appeared, a summer lady on Mt. Desert Island played it one day for the little Butler boy. Afterwards he went home and told his mother he had just heard *Bert and I*.
>
> "Oh," she said, "I hear that's quite a record. What did you think of it?"

He said, "Wel-l-ll, if it's really about Maine, why don't they call it *Me and Bert?*"

Everyone knows the categories of people in the state today. There are the natives and the biscuits, the old-time "rusticators" and the new "summer people." There are tourists, and then there are visitors (both referred to as "summer complaints"). "Year-round summer people" are the rusticators who settled down and stayed. Any license plate from away is "foreign."

I know I will always be "from away," as any native can spot the minute I open my mouth. Most of my Boston vowels are long gone, but I have to reach for the dictionary when I need to write *resevoir*. Or is it *reservoir*? For a document I sign or a wall I'm erecting, is it a *petition*? I confess to be one of those folks Sandy Phippen identifies as people from away who cherish the Maine dialect. Ah, but he happily cherishes it too. It saddens me to hear these dialects fading, or existing only as the medium of comic stories or—worse—commercial jokes. Scott Simon on National Public Radio recently played for a laugh when he put on a Boston accent: "Boston has a lot more cahs than pahking lots." OK. I confess I laughed—and jotted it down.

Oh, well, I trust I can still go down to the fishermen's hangout in Winter Harbor early in the morning, sit quietly with my coffee, and just listen.

APPENDIX A

UNIVERSITY OF MAINE STUDENT SPELLINGS:
1946–1948

Here is the record from the back of my grade books at the University of Maine, 1946-1948. I recognize today that it is a goldmine of how unselfconscious Maine speakers handled the *r* back then. When it might be helpful I add the dictionary spelling in brackets.

helta-skelta
patten [pattern]
petruding
ballard singer
headquaters
stubbon
ochestra
barstard or barstid
ochids
creamer tarter biscuits
surpose to be
coon [croon] to the baby
Chiner
want [weren't] it cold, though?
Joseph Starlin
potable duck blind
gordy colors
to cork [caulk] a boat
carm and collected
mummering brook
portencial

idear
cultervate
insurbordination
mordern, modren, & morden
oppertunity, orpertunity
illerstraight
wobbling birds [warbling]
dillemer
norminal
town farthers
squarbell [squabble]
advercate
differculty
penertrate
short down over the Pacific
supprising
parculiar
pecarious
silver-culture
corsarge
fundermantle

— 58 —

povity

ripperling waters

parephernalia

wiltered flowers

peppimint

dance a poker

surburban

elergy

strawberry shot-cake

critercise

lobster shots

suffercate, suffercating

intergrated

mental prowress

cornception

warble [wobble]

You ride in gondolers in Venus and see dirty little Warps in the streets.

interlectual & interlectural

disintergrate

orperating

coorporate

The state of Vaginia

Orthello

perculiarly

propagander, properganda

invertation

Louisa Rolcott

experdition

squarted in a blind

## APPENDIX B
### KATHERINE HEIDINGER, "TRANSPLANT TRANSLATES OUR DIALECT FOR TOURISTS"

When Katherine Heidinger, a native Mississippian, moved to Hancock County in the seventies, she suffered from a mighty communication gap. For the *Ellsworth American* (9 August 1979) she compiled this dictionary to help other folks from away make the adjustment. Like other columnists for the *Ellsworth American*, Esther Wood, Hale Joy, and Bill Benson, she is interested in colloquial diction as well as pronunciation; she has a good ear, and her column is worth reproducing for its record of coastal language in the seventies.

[Notes in square brackets are mine.]

Wintah Habbah: Lovely coastal town across Frenchman's Bay from sistah Bah Habbah and Mount Desert (pronounced as in lemon pie or banana pudding) Island. [There was for years a Bordeaux Dairy on MDI that put "Mount Dessert" as the address on its cartons. And some locals pronounce it desert, consistent in meaning if not in sound with Samuel de Champlain's *Isle des Monts Déserts*, meaning barren.]

Stow-ah: Usually refers to a business establishment, i.e. food, clothing, drugstore (without drugs) or five and dime.

Cleck: One who works behind the counter in a Stow-ah.

Hasses: Animals to ride, work, feed or shovel up after. Hasses have manes, hooves, and swishy tails.

Sar: Verb; past tense of to see.

Clar: Another verb. What a cat does to a dog's eyes.

Fierce: Adjective describing enthusiasm as in fierce to hunt, fierce to fish. Bears in Maine are black, not fierce. People in Maine are fierce.

Summah People: Outsider, or furriner. Oftentimes natives speak of year-round summah people, meaning outsiders who have moved to Maine for good.

Wicked: Adjective meaning a lot, or a heap. Usage: The beach was wicked crowded, or these shoes are wicked easy on your feet.

Cunnin': Refers mostly to babies; obviously a compliment. Does not mean foxy but precious, cute, adorable.

Ugly: Disposition only. Not used to describe how homely one is.

Ole Beauties: Wide usage. May refer to two women walking down the street. Can just as easily be used for any item. For example, heard in conversation: "How are you going to carry them candybars on your bicycle?" Answer: "Well, sir, I'm gonna put them ole beauties right in my hip pocket."

Hee-yah: Where you are standing when you're not over They-ah.

Shot: (1) What kids fear from a doctor; (2) What some folks drink in a small glass before, during, or after dinner; (3) What Maine fishermen hate to find when measuring lobsters. A shot lobster which they cannot haul is one that is not long enough.

Flatlandah: Visitor, rusticator, out-of-stater, summah people, or genrally, damn tourist.

To Home: Where you stay if you choose not to go out. [Back in the nineteenth century Oliver Wendell Holmes asked "When is charity like a top?" Answer: "When it begins to hum."]

Cah: Term befitting anything from a Chevy to a Volks to a Mercedes.

Spleeny: Adjective directed at sissies who get cold even in August.

Show-ah: Place at the water's edge where you slip on the rocks and seaweed, find treasures to take back home or feast on steamed lobsters and clams.

Shoe-ah: Means certainly, you're right or I agree.

Scale: Not necessarily what one does to a fish before frying. Can mean to throw away as in "Why don't you just scale that ole beauty and get a new one."

Heist: You can either heist your rear up on that boat or you can take a heist, or fall, over the side. Either usage is correct in Maine.

Dungy: Tired, groggy, before your two cups of coffee in the morning.

Gawmy: Clumbsy or awkward. No one should leave the house if he's feeling both dungy and gawmy.

Thickafog: One word meaning that Egg Rock foghorn will be bellowing till the wind changes. Thickafog in Winter Harbor is thicker than clam chowder.

Herds: Any amount of anything. One can have herds of money, see herds of swimmers at the pond, or hunt herds of deer on the island.

Dandy: A favorite word meaning all's well with the world.

Drar: To take a pencil or chalk and sketch a picture. For raffles, someone also drars the winning number.

Dooryard: Area surrounding one's house. You tie your dog there, plant flowers or even park your car.

Abed: Where a Mainer goes to sleep. Usage, "It's 8:30 and I'm going abed."

Conundrum: A puzzle or mystery.

Howl: To cry or even to sniffle. No youngster in Maine cries when punished and no wife gets teary when watching "Little House on the Prairie." They howl.

Do not panic when someone sucks in his chest, gasps, and says, "Ay-up." His pacemaker has not failed. Nor do you need to administer the bear hug method for choking victims. He is merely answering your dumb question in the affirmative.

## PRINCIPAL SOURCES

I have indicated published sources as I've gone along, but among my sixty years' collection of loose clippings, memos scribbled while riding in a car, goodies sent me by alert friends, and notes deposited in my memory bank are many I'd be hard pressed to date accurately. I consider them covered by what the Association of American Publishers' Rights and Permissions Advisory Committee considers "fair use"—"certain uses of excerpts from a work for purposes such as comment, criticism, or study." All the originals will be deposited with the Northeast Archives of Folklore and Oral History at the Maine Folklife Center in Orono.

I published a short essay on the Orono material: Marion Kingston [now Stocking], "I got the idear," *Colorado Quarterly*, Spring, 1953, pp. 415-19. It was reprinted and excerpted here and there at the time. *The New England Teacher* published an expurgated version; words like *corpulating* had to go so as not to offend the parochial school teachers who subscribed.

Here are my principal sources for the present work:

Bill Benson, columns ("Island Watch"), *Ellsworth American*, 1990s.
Earl Brechlin, columns ("From This Corner"), *Ellsworth Weekly*, 1996.
William Carpenter. *The Wooden Nickel*. Boston and New York: Little, Brown and Company, 2002.
Paul Doiron, "Is Maine Losing Its Accent?" *Down East*, September, 2001, pp. 62-3.
Carolyn T. Daniels. *Facts and Fancies and Repetitions about Dark Harbor.* Privately printed: 1935.
John Gould, columns and features over many years in *The Christian Science Monitor, Ellsworth Weekly* ("Observations on Maine"), and *Down East*.

———. *Maine Lingo: Boiled Owls, Billdads, and Wazzats.* Camden, Maine: Down East Books, 1975.

Katherine Heidinger, "Transplant Translates Our Dialect for Tourists," *Ellsworth American*, 9 August 1979.

James A. Herne, *Shore Acres.* In *American Drama*, ed. Alan S. Downer. New York: Thomas Y. Crowell, 1960.

Hale Joy, columns ("Just Pondering"), *Ellsworth American*, 1970s, 1980s, and 1990s.

Stephen King. "The Reach." In *Skeleton Cove.* New York: G.P. Putnam's Sons, 1985.

Hans Kurath. *Linguistic Atlas of New England.* Providence, Rhode Island: Brown University, 1939, 1941, 1943.

Gerald E. Lewis. *How to Talk Yankee: A Guide for Tourists, Migrants, and Summer Complaints.* Thorndike, Maine: The Thorndike Press, 1979.

Ruth Moore. *The Walk Down Main Street.* New York: William Morow and Company, 1960. Reprinted Nobleboro, Maine: Blackberry Press, 1988.

———. *When Foley Craddock Tore Off My Grandfather's Thumb: The Collected Stories of Ruth Moore and Eleanor Mayo.* Nobleboro, Maine: Blackberry Press, 2004.

Roorbach, Bill. *Temple Stream: A Rural Odyssey.* New York: Dial Press, 2005.

E.B. White. *One Man's Meat.* Thorndike, Maine: The Thorndike Press, 2000, and various earlier editions.

Esther Wood, columns ("The Native"), *Ellsworth American*, 1970s and 1980s.

AFTERWORD: DIALECTS OF MAINE[1]

by Pauleena MacDougall

> A Babylonish dialect
> Which learned pedants much affect.
> —Samuel Butler *Hudibras*, pt. 1 [1663], canto, 1, 93

> Since our concern was speech, and speech impelled us
> To purify the dialect of the tribe.
> —Thomas Stearns Eliot *Four Quartets*, Little Gidding, II.

Wherever one travels throughout the English-speaking world, one will notice that people have different words for things or different meanings for familiar words and different pronunciations of words. Sometimes it is quite difficult to understand a speaker, even if he or she is speaking American English. These differences in speech pique our curiosity, or may even be a source of humor. When one hears certain words, phrases or pronunciations, an image of a regional American culture comes to our mind's eye. Many American authors have used dialects in their writings to convey a sense of region; for example, the Mississippi dialect in Mark Twain's *Huckleberry Finn*, and Sarah Orne Jewett's writings about Maine. People in Maine hold a great affection for local dialect stories, rhymes and anecdotes. As a matter of fact, storytelling and the real or affected dialect of "Downeast" Maine continues to amuse the public, as testified by the popularity of the "Bert and I" recordings (by Marshall Dodge, born in Brooklyn, New York, but speaking a Wiscasset, Maine dialect); Tim Sample's stand-up humor, and books like *How To Talk Yankee: A Guide for Tourists, Migrants and Summer Complaints* by Gerald E. Lewis (Thorndike Press, 1979). Traveling around the state, stopping at a general store here and there, one will find locally produced recordings of storytelling by the local humorist who repeats the "yarns" using terms like "gorry" and "ayuh" to the delight of the summer people. Why and how did Maine speech develop such a distinctive dialect?

Dialects are simply mutually intelligible forms of a language that differ in systematic ways. All languages change, but dialect differences are commonly the result of change taking place at different rates in different places. Eventually, over great time depth, a dialect will become a new language.

There are many mistaken beliefs about American English dialects. For example, although it is commonly believed, it is not true that people of a given area (Appalachia) speak a pure Elizabethan English, or that people in some parts of the country speak "bad" English.[ii] But Appalachian English does contain some relics of older English no longer in use in other parts of North America.[iii] This is also the case in Maine, especially in small fishing communities where people have little interaction with other parts of the United States. Certain items of vocabulary, as well as pronunciation, grammar and expressions are used within small, close-knit communities. Just as families sometimes have particular vocabulary and expressions, so do small communities and even neighborhoods in large cities. Therefore if someone travels to Maine from, say, New York City, that person encounters speech patterns they are not familiar with.

In an older and more elitist society dialects were considered to be representations of the uncultivated and uneducated. Much dialect humor preserves this stereotype even today. Students at the University of Maine sometimes find their speech the butt of jokes. Teachers frequently try to "correct" their language, marking it ungrammatical or nonstandard. Much of the feeling about the relationship between standard American speech and local dialects is still among us. But what is the standard and who sets it? That too, varies from one part of the country to another. No one, anywhere, actually speaks standard English in a "pure" form. Boston has one standard, the Midwest another and California yet another.

Languages change at different rates and in different places. Let's imagine that a community of English speakers from Bristol,

England, came to Maine and half of them settled in eastern Maine and half of them in southern Maine. Assuming little contact between them, the English spoken in these two communities two hundred years later would be different. One community would retain some relics of the old speech. The other community would probably retain some different vocabulary. That is why someone in eastern Maine might use the term "toll" for bait used to entice mackerel, while someone in another part of the state might use a different term. Now suppose that another group of immigrants came from Bristol, England, to settle in one of these communities two hundred years later. They, too, would speak a different dialect with different vocabulary, pronunciation and grammar from the two earlier immigrant communities. This is the way it works in living languages at all times. Some major events can drastically change speech communities (war, pestilence, large immigrations of foreigners). But even without drastic change, speech communities' languages change with every generation. That is why linguists generally reject the notion that there is a "correct" way of speaking English, though most English teachers would strongly disagree.

The idea that the earliest American colonists spoke "Elizabethan English" among themselves has minimal accuracy, because there were more varieties of English than one when the language was brought to America. According to linguist J.L. Dillard, "It does not appear that there were much more than chance affinities between the English of the earliest colonists and that of leading Elizabethan literary figures like Shakespeare." Dillard cites usage such as *it dislikes me*, *it yearns me* and *methinks* found in Shakespeare's plays but not found in early American English. This is also true of the English dialect reflected in the King James translation of the Bible, which was probably more readily available to colonists than Shakespeare.[iv]

As Dillard argues, all British immigrants to the Americas encountered a linguistically complicated situation. The Puritans may have been the most homogeneous group to arrive in New England, but their journey was complicated. They began in Nottinghamshire, but first went to Leyden, Holland. They began to assimilate with the Dutch and their children began marrying the Dutch so by the time the Mayflower went to New England, they were hardly speaking a pure English dialect any longer.[v]

Later, Boston became a great commercial port, shipping and trading with the West Indies, the Madeiras and Canary Islands, the Native Americans, Newfoundland, Africa and China. Maritime trade was the principle economic activity and as a result, the greatest influence on language and culture. In addition, whereas so many immigrants came to America seeking religious freedom, religion, too, had some effect on American English, particularly in terminology (i.e. "prayer meeting").

What happened next in American speech is something linguists call "leveling." It is the process whereby children of Americans put pressure on immigrant children to speak as they do, making life miserable for them if they used a foreign word. So, while the birth of American speech took place in diversity, Dillard explains that the effect of leveling led to the adoption of Americanisms by all of the colonists in a fairly short time.[vi] According to Dillard, American speech was highly diverse in the first two decades of the eighteenth century, but then the process of leveling occurred so that by the American Revolution, all of the colonies were speaking an American English that was relatively uniform.[vii] All of this would change, however, as another process occurred, that of regionalization.

Regionalization began as Americans began to colonize and settle in great numbers over the face of the continent. While some of the settlers were of New England stock, many were immigrants. These immigrants went through the process of leveling, but not without first adding their own colors to the fabric of American speech.

The Germans settling in Pennsylvania, for example, influenced English there with phrases such as "leave me be" where the term *leave* replaces *let*, as both words are expressed in German with the term *lassen*.[viii] In the south, both Scots-Irish and African American (especially Caribbean and pidgin) influences appear. In the Gulf region, Native American, African, French and Spanish all color the local English speech. In the west, the language of cowboys was strongly influenced by Spanish. But everywhere the process of regionalization of speech was much more complicated than I have indicated here. Occupations, other immigrant groups, and innovations all created changes in pronunciation, vocabulary and usage. However, due to the mobility of Americans and more recently, the introduction of radio and television and other media, American speech has adopted some of these regional usages as part of the mainstream in a process known as de-regionalization. Regionalization was clearly recognizable throughout the U.S. by the 1880s. However events such as World War I and II that influenced mobility and population redistribution leveled many of these regional distinctions.

### MAINE

The development of Maine dialects is the result of many very complex factors. The history of the settlement of Maine provides the first clue to Maine speech. The earliest inhabitants of Maine were the Native people. Their languages belong to the great Algonquian family of North America. Maine's culture and its language owe much to the people who speak Penobscot, Passamaquoddy and Maliseet. A large number of words have come into American English from Algonquian languages (for example, words like *toboggan* and *skunk*). Some examples that are unique to Maine are *pokelogan* or *logan*, "a false inlet that often traps logs during a log drive," or *wangan*, "the place of stores of foodstuffs and other essentials for logging companies." The earliest Europeans to arrive in Maine influenced Maine English dialects as well. The Basques, the French and the English sent fishermen to Maine's waters for cod. Later still the French and English arrived on shore to trade for furs and eventually to colonize the land. One term used in literature about Maine appears to be of Basque origin: *Tarrentine*, a term used by early historians for the Micmacs or mistakenly for the Penobscots.[ix] The French left their mark on the landscape as well with place names such as Acadia,[x] and Mount Desert Island[xi] and with common terms such as for portage, "a carry."

Occupation, religion, and social class also influence dialects. Many of Maine's unique expressions and vocabulary derive from farming, fishing and boatbuilding occupations (i.e.: "numb as a hake, slick as a smelt," the use of the term "toll" for bait that is spread on the waters (from the meaning, to entice or to lure) and "dressing" for manure put on the garden.

In the seventeenth century, Maine's English settlers came from the West Country, London, interior England, and the Bay Colony. They were primarily farmers, fishermen and small townspeople. Anglicans, Puritans, Antinomians[xii] and Quakers settled mostly in southern and western Maine. Some were Scots and Scots-Irish. We find vestiges of broad Scots dialect in terms such as "ayuh" (aye), and "sten" meaning an allotment of work. The term "dight" used to denote a small amount of something (often a helping of food) is a relic of Middle English.

Other terms may derive from other early settlers in Eastern Maine such as the French Huguenots and Catholics who mostly engaged in the fur trade in alliances with Wabanaki people. In the first centuries of European settlement, conflict between France and England continued for many years. The English eventually ruled over eastern Maine when they defeated the French in 1763. After the American Revolution, from about 1783 to 1861 a great influx of immigrants from Southern New England, New Hampshire, England and Ireland peopled Maine's landscape.[xiii]

The eastern area of Maine was largely settled by farmers from eastern Massachusetts with a scattering of Irish. Much of northern Maine was settled by the Acadian French, while most of the larger numbers of French Canadians and Irish arrived after 1840. However, I believe the greatest impact on Maine's dialects came from the interaction of Maine families with other parts of the world during the eighteenth and nineteenth centuries, when many families went to sea. This idea is based on the observation that each of the four geographically separated areas on the Atlantic seaboard now lacking postvocalic /r/ (when the r disappears after a vowel as in Hahvahd for Harvard) had one or more prominent seaports (Boston, New York, Richmond, Charleston) through which close contacts with England were maintained.[xiv] The people of southern England mainly speak with an r-less dialect.

This very brief synopsis of Maine's early immigration ignores much diversity and some ethnic groups. However, the majority of the earliest Maine immigrants' ancestors were from the British Isles and France. It is from the English stock that the Maine dialect descends—but with numerous additions from Native and immigrant languages.

In a state as large as Maine, with an immigration history spanning five hundred years, you might expect more than one dialect of English to be spoken here. And so it is. Not all Mainers say *idear*. Not all Mainers use terms like *gorry* and *ayuh*. Not everyone is a laconic farmer or fisherman. Some of the pronunciations and usages found in Maine that are stereotypically "Downeast" are relics from earlier times. Others are innovations.

The people of Maine seem to love to play with their language. Many of the sayings heard are similes that refer to aspects of nature, religion or human behavior. For example, "As polite as a basket of chips, worse than the seven-years' itch, mad enough to bite off a board nail, frisky as a colt, wild as a heifer (usually referring to a teenage girl with hormones raging), greener than a gosling, common as dog's tracks, uneasy as a boiled dish, sowed thicker than spatters, or thicker than a hair on a dog." "He can lie faster than a horse can trot, no bigger than a pint of cider, homelier than a sheared sheep, dry as a contribution box, poor as Job's turkey, smart as a steel trap, plumper than a partridge." Additionally, one may hear "red as a boiled lobster, dull as a hoe, full as a tick," and many, many more.[xv]

Linguists differ in how they account for Maine speech. The earliest students of Maine dialects believed they were relics of certain English dialects. More recent linguists suspect a much more complex evolution. A review of some of the major studies may shed some light on the topic.

Some of the earliest dialect fieldwork began under the direction of Hans Kurath in 1929 for a proposed Linguistic Atlas of the United States and Canada. Lack of funds caused by the Depression and two World Wars resulted in the publication of only the *Linguistic Atlas of New England*.[xvi] Although a large amount of data has been collected, most of Maine's dialects are swept into the larger designation of New England as if it were a single dialect. Linguists describe the New England dialect as non-rhotic, meaning that speakers drop r's after vowels. This area is further subdivided into Eastern New England, including Boston and much of Maine, where [o] and [au] shift into an intermediate vowel so that the vowels in *cot* and *caught* are merged. Transitional between Eastern New England and New York, Western New England is less well defined.

On these two topics, the non-rhotic and the vowel /o/, much has been written. In an article titled "The Phonology of New England English," C.K. Thomas wrote:

> The treatment of /r/ before a consonant or a pause is one of the traditional characteristics of New England speech, the western area retaining [r], the eastern replacing it with added vowel length, or in some contexts, with [r]. In Maine we find [r] retained in Aroostook County while the rest of Maine are consistently without [r]. In cloth, coffee, cough, cross, lost, and sausages, [au] predominates in most parts of New England but in Maine, it is pronounced [a].[xvii]

Bernard Bloch discovered speech islands in Maine, notably a cluster of isolated villages along the sparsely settled coast of eastern Maine where the /r/ is pronounced, although generally, eastern New England speakers tend to drop their /r/s—and western New England speakers (west of the Connecticut River) tend to pronounce them after vowels.[xviii]

Many visitors have noticed the pronunciation of the /o/ in words like boat, as if it were two short vowels [boət], as opposed to the pronunciation of /o/ in rode, which does not have the diaphonic feature and in which the /o/ is lengthened. This usage is not found throughout Maine, however. Walter Avis wrote, as an explanation for their dialect differences with the rest of Maine, that Fort Fairfield (which pronounces its /o/s as a single long vowel like western New England) is a town settled by Loyalists from New Jersey and New York at the time of the Revolutionary War and moreover is culturally and economically oriented toward New Brunswick, rather than New England. Fort Kent speech also reflects Canadian dialect, but has much more French influence because it was first settled by Acadian French. Further south, in Waldoboro and Nobleboro there is another enclave of speakers who use the monopthong /o/ resulting from their German and Scots-Irish background. He relates that this use of the /o/ and the post-vocalic /r/ are characteristic of the speech of New Brunswick and generally of Scotch-Irish settlements in the Eastern United States.[xix]

However, another author described the similarities between dialects of eastern New England and Standard British English in lacking the postvocalic /r/ and he attributes this to the close contacts with England through the prominent seaport of Boston.[xx]

More recent studies have taken a different approach. Rather than looking for explanations for New England regional speech in England, they have reviewed early American culture and the influences of diversity on American speech. The result is a theory that New England dialects derive from the lingua franca (that is, a trade language derived from the contact of languages sometimes called *pidgin*) of seafaring folk who interacted with coastal New England for most of its developmental history.

Maine writer Joanna Colcord hinted at this explanation in her book *Sea Language Comes Ashore*.[xxi] The American word *lingo* she says, "was brought home from the Mediterranean where 'lingua franca,' a mixture of several tongues, is generally used." She also traced the term *savvy* to Spanish *sabe* (though it more probably comes from Portuguese). In Maine a term like no-see-'em is a survival from a pidgin derived from (Algonquian-English) describing a minute biting fly or midge. Thoreau published the word in 1848 and the word made its way to the speech of the Pacific coast of North America by 1949.[xxii]

Dillard described the language situation during the period of European colonial expansion as "greatly different." He portrayed the nearly universal use of a lingua franca. English traders developed a Pidgin English from the lingua franca that had an Iberian base (primarily Portuguese), adopting numerous words from pidgins they encountered. It is not difficult to see how Pidgin English could spread rapidly along trade routes. Dillard cites a 1784 example from Massachusetts' records of Pidgin English use by Chinese traders in Boston.[xxiii] He concludes that trade, contact or marginal languages were employed by the European sailors who did the actual work of geographical exploration for some time, and they were in constant contact with other languages, which led to numerous innovations. The Maritime English of sailors is a much better candidate for contributions to American English dialects, because it represents the kind of multilingual contact that was characteristic of the colonial period in English and American history. In addition, the earliest British colonists were involved in sea trade. Sailors were at home and close to the Americans ashore. They were involved in whaling, slaving and rum trade until the development of the west after 1850.[xxiv] Even during the gold rush, fleets of American ships went to California ports from New England. It seems reasonable to propose that the influence of Maritime English, with its many foreign flavors, had the greatest influence on American English in New England (including Maine) before 1850.

Whatever its history, the Maine dialect consists of interesting turns of phrase, unique usage, and vocabulary. E.B. White noted a few of these "peculiarities" in *One Man's Meat*. Some of the differences he noted between the vocabulary of the people of Brooklin, Maine and his own (mid-Atlantic) dialect relate to usage: "the whole of it" for all, "heft" for lift, "tunk" for hammer (verb), "spleeny" for someone sensitive to the cold. As for pronunciation, it is the combination of –[ar]- in a word that is pronounced [ae] that gave him the most trouble "famine" [faemən] for farming, for example, and the pronunciation of the final –y- [i]of a word as "ay" [e] Fredday, for Freddie.

So many maritime words and phrases pepper Maine speech, that it is not surprising that westerners or southerners not familiar with these terms would have difficulty understanding *abeam*, *adrift*, or "two lamps burning and no ship at sea."

Scholarly understanding of Maine dialects is paltry. Jacob Bennett, emeritus Professor at the University of Maine, published research about one Maine dialect in Kittery Point, Maine,[xxv] and taught a class in the dialects of Maine some years ago. However, no one has ever conducted a systematic study of the dialects of Maine, their history, and how they differ from one region of Maine to another. The rapid changes today resulting from the influx of many immigrants (from elsewhere in the United States as well as from other countries) and radio and television may be difficult, even impossible to document. However, there are still numerous small, somewhat isolated communities in Maine where dialect differences are more pronounced.

In discussing the impact on local dialect of the rapid changes and influx of urban migrants to her home state of Vermont, Audrey R. Duckert wrote:

> And so we must keep track. It is a Yankee way of life, keeping track. The dates of the first snowfall ("enough to track a cat") must be recorded, whether on the barn wall, in a diary, or in a black loose-leaf book like the one Emma Brown kept on top of the refrigerator (which she, of course, called the ice chest) so she'd always know where it was. It is important to continue keeping track of the language and the society that uses it, whose life and living it both reflects and shapes.[xxvi]

i  Thank you to Edward D. "Sandy" Ives, Marion K. Stocking and Jane Smith for reading and commenting on an earlier draft. I take full responsibility for any errors.
ii  See Michael Montgomery "In the Appalachians they speak like Shakespeare," and Dennis R. Preston, "They Speak Really Bad English Down South and in New York City" in *Language Myths*, Laurie Bauer and Peter Trudgill, eds. (New York: Penguin Books, 1998) 66-76, 139-149.
iii  W.N. Francis, *Dialectology: An Introduction* (London and New York: Longman, 1983) 7-9.
iv  J. L. Dillard, *Toward a Social History of American English* (New York: Mouton, 1985) 8.
v  J. L. Dillard *A History of American English* (London and New York: Longman, 1992) 23.
vi  *Toward a Social History of American English*, 63.
vii  *A History of American English*, 34.
viii  *Toward a Social History of American English*, 97.
ix  Frank T. Siebert, Jr. "The Identity of the Tarrantines, with an Etymology," *Studies in Linguistics*. 23 (1973) 69-76.
x  All of New France was called Acadie at one time.
xi  Named by Samuel Champlain Mont Desert.
xii  Antinomians were a Protestant sect who believed that faith alone brought salvation.
xiii  Richard W. Judd, Edwin A. Churchill, Joel W. Eastman, *Maine: The Pine Tree State from Prehistory to the Present* (Orono: University of Maine Press, 1995) 56-57.
xiv  Hans Kurath, "British Sources of Selected Features of American Pronunciation: Problems and Methods," in Harold B. Allen, ed., *Readings in American Dialectology* (New York: Appleton-Century-Crofts, 1971) 267.
xv  Some expressions from Anne E. Perkins "More Notes on Maine Dialect," *American Speech* IV(1929) 118.
xvi  Raven I. McDavid, Jr., "Linguistic Geography," in Harold B. Allen and Michael D. Linn, eds. *Dialect and Language Variation* (New York: Academic Press, Inc., 1986) 118.
xvii  *Readings in American Dialectology*, 61, 64.
xviii  Bernard Bloch, "Postvocalic r in New England Speech, a Study in American Dialect Geography." *Readings in American Dialectology*, 197.
xix  "The "New England Short o": a Recessive Phoneme" *Readings in American Dialectology*, 212.
xx  Hans Kurath, "British Sources of Selected Features of American Pronunciation: Problems and Methods, *Readings in American Dialectology*, 267.

xxi (New York: Cornell Maritime Press, 1945)
xxii Colcord is cited in Dillard, *Toward a Social History of American English*, 27-29.
xxiii *Toward a Social History of American English*, 19.
xxiv *Toward a Social History of American English*, 24
xxv "George Savary Wasson and the Dialect of Kittery Point, Maine" *American Speech* 49 (Spring-Summer, 1974) 54-66; "George Savary Wasson's Approach to Dialect Writing" *American Speech* 54 (Summer, 1979) 90-101.
xxvi "The Speech of Rural New England" in Harold B. Allen and Michael D. Linn, eds. *Dialect and Language Variation* (New York: Academic Press, Inc., 1986) 137.

# INDEX

Alcott, Louisa May, *Little Women*, movie, 1994: Robin Swicord, screenplay; Gillian Armstrong, director, 5
Allen, Fred, 6
Angelhom, 22
*A Vanished World*, 27
Austin, Phyllis, 25
Avis, Walter, 73

Baldacci, John, 38
*Bangor Daily News*, ix, 14, 19, 26
*Bar Harbor Times*, 23, 27, 52
Beem, Edgar Allen, 25
Beloit College, 18
*Beloit Poetry Journal*, 27, back cover
Bennett, Jacob, 34, 75
Benson, Bill, 34–35, 60, 63
Betsy's Kitchen, 22
BIG T CAHDS, 54–55
Birdsacre Sanctuary, 33
Bissett, Virgil, 33
Blackmur, R. P., *Sea Island Miscellany*, 51
Blackstone, Hazel, 26
Bloch, Bernard, 72
Blount, Roy, Jr., 38
Boston Symphony, 8
Bousquet, Don, 53
Brechlin, Earl, xiii, 43–44, 63
Browne, Charles Farrar (Artemus Ward), 10, 43
Bryan, Robert, *Bert and I*, 6
Burns, (Budnz), Robbie, 19

Carpenter, William, xiii; *The Wooden Nickel*, 46, 63
Casco Bay Store, 22
Champlain, Samuel de, *Isle des Monts Déserts*, 60
Chute, Carolyn, x, xiii; *The Beans of Egypt, Maine*, 46
*Christian Science Monitor*, 7
Clemens, Samuel (Mark Twain), *Huckleberry Finn*, 65
Climate Change Institute, 25

Coffin, Robert Peter Tristram, 23
Colcord, Joanna, *Sea Language Comes Ashore*, 73–74
College of the Atlantic, 27
*Colorado Quarterly*, 63
Colorado, University of, 17
Cooperative Extension Service, 23

Daniels, Carolyn T., 3
Day, Holman, ix; *When Egypt Went Broke*, 45
Dickens, Charles, 8
Dick's Corner Store, 21
Dillard, J. L., 67-68, 74
Dodge, Marshall, *Bert and I*, 6, 33, 39, 51, 56, 65
Doiron, Paul, xiii, 39, 43, 63
Donaldson, Kate, 5
*Down East*, 39, 52
Duckert, Audrey R., 75
Duke University, 7, 8

Ellis, Milton, 7
*Ellsworth American*, 14, 21, 22, 25-26, 34–35, 38, 52, 53, 60, 63
*Ellsworth Weekly*, 23, 43, 63
Emerson, Ralph Waldo, 10
Emerson, Lydian (*nee* Lydia Jackson), 10
Emerson, Mary Moody, 10

"Farewell to Tobacco," Charles Lamb, 19–20
Farmington, University of Maine at, 27
Fennelley, Parker (Titus Moody), 6
Fife, Hilda, xiii
Foust, Barbara Kingston, 3
Francoise I, King, 14
Freese's Department Store, 14

Geddy's Pub, 54
Gould, John, ix, xiii, 7, 27, 34; 44, 45; *Maine Lingo*, 35, 44, 47, 56, 63–64
Gramm, Philip, 26
*Guillemot, The*, 27

Hatch, D. H., 35

— 78 —

Heaney, Seamus, 7
Heidinger, Katherine, XII, 60–62, 64
Herne, James A., *Shore Acres*, 43, 64
Holmes, Oliver Wendell, 61
"Humble Farmer, The," see Skoglund, Robert
Humpty Dumpty Nursery School, 23
Hunt, Leigh, 19

Ikemiya, Ysuneko, 19
Institute for Quaternery Studies, 25
Istomin, Eugene, 33
Ives, Edward D. (Sandy), XIII
Ivins, Molly, 19

Jewett, Sarah Orne, 65
Joukovsky, Nicholas A., 19
Joy, George, 25
Joy, Hale, 14, 22, 26, 53, 60, 64

Keats, John, 5, 19
*Keats-Shelley Journal*, 20
*Keats-Shelley Memorial Bulletin*, 19
King, Stephen, x, XIII; "The Reach," 46, 64
Kingston, William Frank, 3
Knights of Theropolae (Thermopylae), 25
Kurath, Hans, *Linguistic Atlas of New England*, XI, 31, 64, 72
Kursar, Sylvia M., 23

Lamb, Charles, 19-20
Landau, Martin, 16
Leavitt, Bud, 25
Leavitt, H. Walter, *Katahdin Skylines*, 8
Leeman, Bob, 21, 23
Lewis, Gerald E., *How to Talk Yankee*, 34, 64, 65
Libby, Burt, XIII
Libby, Margaret (Marnie) Balch, XIII
Litton, Masha, 32
Lowell, James Russell, *The Biglow Papers*, 10, 43
Lynch, Kathleen, 16

McDavid, Raven, 31
MacDougall, Pauleena, XIII, IX-X, 65–77
Machias Hospital, 28, 32
Maine Arts Commission, 27

Maine Folklife Center, 63
*Maine Life*, 23
*Maine Organic Farmer and Gardener*, IX, 24
Maine Public Radio, 33
*Maine Times*, IX, 14, 21, 25, 33, 35, 51, 52
Maine, University of, IX, X, XIII, 7, 8, 16, 25, 58, 66, 75
Mather, Mort, 24
Mather, Barbara, 24
Mayo, W. Alan, 23
Melville, Herman, *Moby Dick*, 25
Mitchell, George, 23, 33, 38
Mitchell, Wilmot Brookings, 7
Montale, Eugenio, 39
Moore, Busta, 26
Moore, Harearl (Buzza), 26
Moore, Ruth, xiii, 56; *When Foley Craddock Tore Off My Grandfather's Thumb*, 45; *The Walk Down Maine Street*, 45, 64
Morison, Samuel Eliot, *The European Discovery of America*, 14
Moskal, Jeanne, 20
Moss, Ruth, 53
Mount Holyoke College, IX, 7, 8, 16, 43
Munger, Bruce, 52
Muskie, Edward, 33
*My Fair Lady*, George Bernard Shaw, 37

National Public Radio, 57
Native Maine'ah™, 55
Nault, Marc, 23
*New England Teacher, The*, 63
*New York Times*, 4, 33, 38
*New Yorker*, 33
Nielsen, Nancy, XIII
Northeast Archives of Folklore and Oral History, 19, 63

Ocean House, 22
Oronoka, 22
*Oxford Universal Dictionary*, 19

Peabody, Eddie, 26
Phippen, Sanford (Sandy), XIII, 23, 34; *The Police Know Everything*, 37, 46, 57
Pilot's Grill, 22

Redpath, Jean, 19
Reynolds, Cecil, 12
Richardson, Douglas, 21
Richmond, Chandler, 33
Robb, Margaret, 17
Roorbach, Bill, *Temple Stream*, 47-48
Roosevelt, Franklin Delano, 38
Rowantrees Pottery, 32
Royal Academy of Dramatic Art (RADA), 16

St. Lawrence University, 8
Sample, Tim, 19, 39, 65
Sanderlin, Owenita, 8
*Saturday Evening Post*, 8
Shakespeare, William, 13, 67
Shaw, George Bernard, *Pygmalion*, 37
Shortall, Keith, 33
Simon, Scott, 57
Sing's Polynesian Restaurant, 22
Skoglund, Robert ("The Humble Farmer"), 33
Snowe, Olympia, 25, 26
Sockabasin, Allen, 36
Spenser, Edmund, 8
Stocking, Andrew, xiii, 18
Stocking, Anne, xiii
Stocking, Fred, xiii
Stocking David M., 18

Stone, Marshall L., 34
Sunstein, Emily, 20

Thomas, C. K., 71
Thoreau, Henry David, *The Maine Woods*, 73–74
Townsend, William (Bill), 27–28
*Tuesday Weekly*, 23–24
Twain, Mark (Samuel Clemens), *Huckleberry Finn*, 65

Unobsky's, 21

Verrazzano, Giovani da, 14
Vesalius, Andreas, 33

Walters, Mrs., 6
Ward, Artemus, see Browne, Charles Farrar
*Weekly Shopper*, 21
Welles, Orson, 25
Wellesley College, 8
White, E. B., *One Man's Meat*, 47, 48, 64, 77
Wilson's, 22
Wiggins, James Russell, 51
Wood, Esther, 26, 38, 61, 64

Yerxa, William (Bo) II, 52